STUDIES IN LINGUISTICS:

OCCASIONAL PAPERS

3

GEORGE L. TRAGER and HENRY LEE SMITH, JR.

AN OUTLINE OF ENGLISH STRUCTURE

[Sixth Printing]

Washington

American Council of Learned Societies

1957

FOREWORD TO THE SIXTH PRINTING

At the time of the second printing of this work, in April 1956, it was indicated that it was being reprinted unchanged from the original (1951), except for correction of typographical errors. It was also stated that the authors had arrived at many changes in their conclusions in the morphemics chapter, and had greatly expanded their treatment of syntax and metalinguistics. These statements were repeated in the third, fourth, and fifth printings.

The hoped-for writing of a completely revised *English structure* has not come to pass. The fifth printing being now exhausted, it has been decided to make another printing, to meet the continued demand for copies. But users are urged to remember the original date of publication, to search out the comparatively few publications that have appeared since then which stem from the same analytical foundation, and to use the book's conclusions not as the final word on anything but as points of departure for further analyses.

January, 1965.

[Sixth printing, January, 1965]

LITHOGRAPHED IN THE UNITED STATES OF AMERICA
BY THE GRAPHIC ARTS PRESS, INC.

20

PREFACE

There has long existed a need for a description of English that will be acceptable as the best currently available, and that can serve as a basis for a series of textbooks for teaching English to foreign speakers. Such a need was asserted by the sub-committee on the analysis of English of the Committee on the Language Program of the American Council of Learned Societies (ACLS Bulletin No. 42, March 1949, p.66). There are also needed suitable training materials for those who might undertake to teach English as a second language. The present work was begun by the authors in an attempt to satisfy these needs as they arose in their work with United States government personnel assigned to English teaching and other activities, and coming to the Foreign Service Institute of the Department of State as students.

The authors--claiming only to present the best scientific analysis at their command--welcome the publication of this study in its present form, so that it may be made available for the widest possible comment and criticism by linguistic scientists. They feel that this can justify the use already being made of the material in the preparation of English-teaching texts by the Committee on the Language Program for and at the expense of the Department of State.

To the members of the Committee and to all others responsible for the appearance of this work in print we extend our thanks. We also wish to commend the printers, the Battenburg Press, for their work on the difficult composition involved. For all errors, in proofreading or otherwise, we alone take responsibility.

George L. Trager
Henry Lee Smith, Jr.

Foreign Service Institute, Department of State
Washington, D.C., February 15, 1951

CONTENTS

INTRODUCTION

0. This Outline is intended to serve a two-fold purpose. It exemplifies a methodology of analysis and presentation that we believe to be representative of the scientific method as applied to a social science--linguistics; and it sets forth a series of conclusions about English structure that constitute, in our opinion, the basis for further study and discussion.

The version here given is an extensive reworking of previous drafts (two of Part I--Phonology, and one of Parts II--Morphology and III--Syntax). The preliminary drafts were reproduced in lithoprinted form and distributed to numerous colleagues; comments and criticisms from many of these, as well as collaborative criticism at all stages by other members of the staff of the Foreign Service Institute, have made possible the present statement. The actual writing was done by the named authors.

0.1. No discussion is given of previous work or of differing analyses and conclusions. We put forth this analysis as the report of a series of scientific observations; we have found that the conclusions work, being consistent and furnishing sound bases for further analysis and observation.

For convenience, however, the principal pertinent studies, most of which have extensive bibliographies, are listed:

G.L. Trager and B. Bloch. The syllabic phonemes of English. Language 17.223-46 (1941).

B.L. Whorf. Phonemic analysis of the English of Eastern Massachusetts. SIL 2.21-40 (1943). And: G.L. Trager. Comments on B.L. Whorf, ... SIL 2.41-4 (1943).

Rulon S. Wells. The pitch phonemes of English. Language 21.27-39 (1945).

K.L. Pike. The intonation of American English. Ann Arbor, University of Michigan Press, 1946. xi, 200 p. (University of Michigan Publications, Linguistics 1.)

S.S. Newman. On the stress system of English. Word 2.171-87 (1946).

M. Swadesh. On the analysis of English syllabics. Language 23.137-50 (1947).

K.L. Pike. Grammatical prerequisites to phonemic analysis. Word 3.155-72 (1947).

K.L. Pike. On the phonemic status of English diphthongs. Language 23.151-9 (1947).

0.2. The presentation of the structure of a language should begin, in theory, with a complete statement of the pertinent prelinguistic data. (For this terminology and division of the subject matter, see G.L. Trager, The field of linguistics, SIL:OP1 [March, 1949].) This should be followed by an account of the observed phonetic behavior, and then should come the analysis of the phonetic behavior into the phonemic structure, completing the phonology. The next step is to present the recurring entities--composed of one or more phonemes--that constitute the morpheme list, and go on to their analysis into the morphemic structure. In that process the division into morphology and syntax is made. After the syntax, one may go on from the microlinguistics (linguistics proper--phonology and morphemics) to metalinguistic analyses.

In the present outline prelinguistic data will be largely omitted. Phonetic details will be given at considerable length, though it is not possible to be even reasonably complete within the compass of a work of this kind. However, the material is generally fairly well known in its grosser form, and English-speaking readers can easily fill in the gaps. It is explicitly asserted, moreover, that the procedure with omission of much phonetic data is a practical one for the immediate purpose, and not the theoretically most desirable one that would be followed in a full discussion. The analyses, like any scientific analyses, are based on classifications of behavior events (the occurrence of phonetic material). Syntax, as yet only begun (as will become evident) is necessarily treated sketchily. Metalinguistic analysis is only hinted at at the end of the Outline.

0.3. A problem involved in any analysis of the kind here given is that of stating the extent of validity of the observations and conclusions. We have, over the period of the last 12 years, observed and examined, individually, together, and with many collaborators, a large number of speakers of English from widely distributed regions of the English-speaking world. Included were: Americans from all parts of the United States, Canadians from Eastern, Central, and Western Canada; Australians, New Zealanders; natives of Great Britain--speakers of Southern British, various British provincial speakers, Scotch speakers; speakers from Ireland and various British colonial regions; South Africans. Standard and various types of non-standard speakers were heard for many of these regions. Naturally, careful observation and analysis have been made chiefly for American, Canadian, and Southern British speakers, but all the regional proveniences mentioned have been heard with the analytical frame of reference in mind. The analyses presented are based on these extensive observations, and are intended to be statements of the structure of the English language as a whole, with variation as stated.

It must be recalled in this connection that language is a societal phenomenon. The language of one speaker--an idiolect--is therefore necessarily and by definition incomplete, since at least two speakers (one of whom may be imaginary) are involved in every normal communicational situation. All linguistic description is based on observation of more than one speaker. The extent of validity varies in different languages: for English it is found that the analysis to be presented holds for as much of the system as any one idiolect includes, and for all the systems of all the patterns of idiolects--dialects--that we have observed. By extrapolation it is stated to be the analysis for the total pattern of all the dialects.

PART I: PHONOLOGY

1. We begin with a series of statements presenting the results of phonetic observations. The results are systematized in a way that the original raw data never are at first. In field observation, of course, one sometimes misses a great many data and one has all the language thrown at one, as it were, on all levels at once. But as soon as systematization begins one starts looking for items to fill in gaps. Here we have filled in the gaps and completed the systematization.

The phonetic transcriptions (in brackets) used are based on the general phonetic data presented in chapter 2 of Bloch and Trager, Outline of linguistic analysis (LSA, 1942), and the symbols given or suggested there. The vowels are (only pertinent symbols are included):

	Front		Central		Back	
	Unrounded	Rounded	U	R	U	R
High	[i		ɨ	u̇		u
Lower high	I		ᵻ	U̇	Ï	ʊ
Higher mid	e					o
Mean mid	E		ə		Ë	Ω
Lower mid	ɛ		ɜ		ʌ	ɔ
Higher low	æ					ω
Low	Æ		a		ɑ	ɒ]

By definition the cardinal vowels in the high, higher mid, lower mid, and low rows are tense, the others lax. Modifications are shown by the following symbols: [^] raised, [˔] lowered, [<] advanced, [>] retracted; [˛] nasalized; [̯] offglide or onglide (non-syllabic); [:·˘˘] degrees of length from long to rather long to somewhat long to short; [ₙ] tense, [ᵤ] lax, [ₐ] voiceless, [ɚ] midcentral retroflex.

Consonants are shown by these symbols: [p t k b d g f θ s š v ð z ž m n ŋ l] with their usual cardinal values when unmodified; [ʻ] aspirated release, [˺] unreleased,

[ː] long, [˘] extra short, [ʰ] voiceless onglide or off-glide, [ś] prepalatal, [ʂ] retroflex, [ˢ] affrication ([č ǰ] unanalyzed affricates), [ₔ] vowel timbre, [ₓ] velarized, [ᵧ] palatalized, [P T K] voiceless lenis, [ṭ] voiced fortis, [ʔₜ] glottal stop with secondary apical articulation,[r¹] flap, [ŋ̩] syllabic, [n¹] flapped nasal, [ŋ̆ᵍ] terminally denasalized, [ɹ] non-fricative tongue-retraction spirant, [ɹ₊] the same with friction noise.

Symbols for stresses and pitches, as well as certain other phenomena, are devised *ad hoc* and presented as needed.

1.1. Let us examine the vowels of the following set of English lexical items, pronounced in isolation:

bit bid bin hiss his.

The vowel quality is in each case lower high front unrounded: [ɪ]. In *bit* there is the shortest vowel, in *his* the longest for most speakers; *bid* and *bin* have fairly long vowels too--some speakers having the longest varieties here, sometimes even with a drawling off-glide effect; in *hiss* the vowel is longer than in *bit*, but considerably shorter than in *his* or *bid*; in *bin* there is marked nasalization of the vowel (and some speakers have here a rather lower quality, some having indeed another quality--see below). These variations could be symbolized thus:

[ɪ] [ɪ·] [ɪ̨·] [ɪ̆ː] [ɪː]

Instead of [ɪ̨·] one might find, as stated, [ɪ̨˅·]. For the whole set there are regional variations in tenseness (though this vowel quality is generally lax), and in retraction toward a vowel of quality [ɨ].

The next set of items is:

bet bed Ben mess fez

Here the vowel is mean mid front unrounded, with the variations:

[E] [E·] [Ȩ·] [Eː̆] [Eː]

The variations in length and offglide drawling noted for [ɪ] occur here also. Some speakers will have for both *bin* and *Ben* a vowel of quality [ɪ˅], others will have [E^]

for both. The nasalization of [ᴇ•] is less than that of [ɪ̨•]. In this matter of the identity for some speakers of *bin* and *Ben*, it must be noted that prelinguistic data are now available confirming the conclusions made by hearers of the language that one hears either in the range of [ɪ] or in that of [ᴇ], not something in between.

The third set of items is:

hat *had* *can* (aux. verb) *Cass* *has*

Here some speakers will have the following:

[æ] [æ•] [æ̨•] [æ̆̇] [æ:]

By [æ] we mean here the cardinal higher low front unrounded lax vowel. Very many American English speakers have exactly this quality in *hat*. Many will have a slightly higher and tenser quality, say [æ^], with some drawling, in *had*, *can*, *has*. Numerous other speakers have a very different quality in *had*, *can*, *Cass*, *has*, namely a lower mid tense vowel, with marked length and centralizing off-glide, [ε^ə̯]. Speakers who have [æ] in *had*, *can*, *Cass*, *has*, will also have [ε^ə̯] in other items, such as *bad*, *can* (noun, and verb 'to put into containers'), *pass*, *jazz;* we examine [ε^ə̯] below. In [æ̨•] there is less nasalization than in [ɪ̨•] and [ᴇ̨•]. In comparing the three qualities so far noted, we see that [ɪ] and [ᴇ] are distributed pretty much in the same way everywhere in English, but [æ] is distinctly limited by some speakers.

We next examine this set:

put *good* *puss*

We find the lower-high back rounded (though the rounding is slight) vowel [ᴜ], in the variations [ᴜ], [ᴜ•], [ᴜ̆̇]. Some speakers will have the same vowel in *room*, nasalized, [ᴜ̨]. In *bosom* or *woozy* will be found examples of [ᴜ•] before a voiced spirant, but usually not as long as in monosyllabic items like *his*, *fez*, *has*. Some speakers have another vowel quality, unrounded, in items of this kind, or, in *room*, have entirely different kinds of nuclei (see below).

Following these, we have the items:

but bud bun bus buzz

Here the quality in most American English is that of a centered back unrounded mean mid vowel, lax: [Ë<] (or [ʌ<̂]); the variations are (using a simplified symbol) [ʌ], [ʌ·], [ʌ̜·], [ʌ̆̇], [ʌ:], in the same pattern as before. In Eastern New England and Southern England the quality is different in most of these items: [a̫>̂]

This leads us to the next set of items:

cot cod Don doff Oz

Here most American speakers have a low lax vowel, central or back depending on region: [ɑ], [ɑ>], [a<], or [a]. In Eastern New England and Southern England the vowel is rounded, [ɒ]; in Scotland it is higher and rounded, [ω].

The vowel [ɒ] is found in non-New England American speech with some speakers in such items as *sorry*, with others in *gloss* 'a translation', *log*, the last vowel of *alcohol*, and elsewhere.

In Eastern New England such items as *coat, road, home, whole* have a vowel that is mid back rounded lax, somewhat centered: [Ω<]. Other speakers often have this in *whole* (especially in phrases like *the whole thing*), *gonna*, and elsewhere in scattered items.

Nearly all American speakers use, in the adverb *just*, a lower high central lax unrounded vowel, [ɨ]. This is found widely distributed in other items also, though erratically: *sister, dinner* in the Southeast; *children* rather widely; instead of [ʌ] in *Tulsa, come* in some regions; in many items in Scotch and Irish speech ('ither', 'mither').

There have so far been found vowel qualities in nine ranges:

[ɪ], [ᴇ], [æ], [ɨ], [ʌ<], [ɑ] to [a], [ʊ], [Ω<], [ɒ] to [ω].

There are three front vowels, three central or back unrounded, three back rounded; three vowels are lower high, three are mean mid, three are higher low or low; all are lax, comparatively short, and vary in length, nasalization, and off-glide in the same way. They are the simple vocalic nuclei.

1.21. We turn now to the complex vocalic nuclei, examining them in the same manner as we have done for the simple ones.

The first set of items is:

seat seed seen cease sees see

We note first variations in length: *seat* has the shortest nucleus, *see* the longest; *sees* has a nucleus almost as long as that of *see*, while *seed* and *seen* are somewhat shorter; *cease* has a short nucleus, but not as short as *seat*. In *seen* there is nasalization. So far, the variation parallels that for the simple nuclei, except that an item like *see* has no parallel in that set.

Turning to the quality of the vocalic nuclei here, we find that there is an onset in raised lower high front position, [ɪ^], with glide upward and forward, ending in high position, [i]; the symbolization [ɪ^i̯] can be adopted, showing onset position and implied glide, with the final position designated by the symbol for non-syllabicity. In *seat* the movement and glide is very rapid and short, in *see* it is very marked. Nowhere do we find a completely static tense long vowel of the type of cardinal [i].

The next set of items is:

late laid lane lace lays lay

Here the length and nasalization are as for [ɪ^i̯]. The quality for most American English begins with [ᴇ] and glides upward and forward, but no higher than to a somewhat tense [ɪ]; variations from [ᴇɪ̯] found regionally are [ᴇ^ɪ̯^] in some Northern Middle Western speakers, [ᴇˇɪ̯] or [ᴇe̯] in some Southern speakers, [ɛɪ̯] in Southern British.

In the items

light lied line lice lies lie

there is a complex nucleus with the quality [ae̯] for most English speakers (both elements being usually lax). In some parts of the Central Atlantic seaboard the first element is back, [ɑe̯]; in Southeastern American it may be much further forward, with a lower final position, [a<ᴇ̯], in such items as *lied*, and with a centered first element, [a^e̯] in such items as *light*. Some Central Atlantic and Irish speakers have a rounded first element, [ɒe̯].

The set of items

Hoyt Lloyd loin choice joys boy

shows a nucleus of the quality [ΩI̯], with well-rounded first element, for most speakers. Some speakers will have lower elements, [ωI̯ˇ], or even [ɒe̯].

In some Southeastern American many speakers have [æe̯] in such items as *hand, pass*. In Philadelphia, and north and south of it for some distance, many speakers have [ɨi̯] in items like *see, seat*, etc. In older-generation New York City speech, and in Charleston, S.C., New Orleans, and elsewhere along the Southern Atlantic coast, many speakers use [ə>I̯] or [ʌ^I̯] in such items as *hurt, heard, nurse* (but rarely in *fur* or *her*). In Southern Middle Western there are speakers who use [ɒe̯] in *wash* and [ʊi̯] in *push* (as also [æe̯] in *ash*).

In each of the complex nuclei examined so far, there is an initial element that falls within the range of the nine qualities found for the simple nuclei--[ɪ^], [E^ E], [æ], [ɨ], [ə> ʌ^], [a< a a^ ɑ], [ʊ], [Ω], [ɒ]--and a final element ranging in height from [E̯] or [e̯] through [I̯] to [i̯], with the height of the terminal element directly related to that of the initial element, so that [E̯ e̯] occur after low vowels, [I̯ I̯^] after mid vowels, and [i̯] after high vowels. There are no other qualities observed in upward-forward gliding complex nuclei.

1.22. Let us now look at the following items:

boot booed boon loose lose do

Here there are complex nuclei which differ in length and nasalization as did those presented in 1.21. The nucleus is kinetic in each case, beginning for much American speech at about [U^], and terminating at about [u̯]. The movement varies from short and slight in *boot* to very marked in *do*. None of these items ever has a static tense long vowel [u]. Regional variations in these items show [ɨʷu̯] and [üu̯].

We go on to the next set:

coat code cone dose doze dough

Here the initial element is in most American English about [ɑ], and the terminal one is [U̯], somewhat tense (the occurrence of [Ω<] alone in *coat*, etc. has been discussed in 1.1). A regional variation (Central Atlantic Coast, Southern England) is [ʌ<U̯] or [əU̯]. In some (mostly British) class-dialects we find [E>u̯], with very little rounding in the terminal element.

In the set of items

bout loud down house rouse now

many American speakers, north and south, have nuclei of the type of [æo̯], with the first element ranging down and back through [Æ] and [a] to [ɑ<]. The latter two get into the range of [ɑo̯], which is most common in the Northern Middle Western and Far Western American dialects, and in British English. In some parts of the American Southern Coastal region items like *house* have [ɛˇȯ̯], with fronted terminal element. In Canada *bout* is likely to have [əˇU̯].

In some Southern (Coastal and interior) speech items like *bought, dawn, cause, law* have a nucleus [ɒo̯]. In some older generation Northern Middle Western items like *cute, cube, abuse* (noun and verb), *few* have [I^u̯].

All the nuclei examined here have initial elements in the ranges of the simple nuclei previously found, and terminal points that are back, higher and more rounded--[u̯], [U̯], [o̯].

1.23. A third kind of complex nucleus remains to be examined. In these the movement from the initial position is always in the direction of mid-central, with the height of the terminal point varying directly again with the height of the onset.

In *idea, theater* many speakers have [I^ɨ̯ˇ]; such a nucleus also occurs occasionally in an item like *bean* (as in Rhode Island). In 'r-less' dialects items like *feared, fierce, fears, fear* have a nucleus of the same type, while in the Eastern and Southern American 'r-pronouncing' dialects these items have a nucleus that is similar but with retraction (or retroflection) at the end--[ɪ^ɨ̭ˇə̽˞].

In *yeah* most speakers have [ɛ^ə̽]. Such a nucleus is also found in items like *bad, pan, pass, jazz* for many speakers (cf. above, 1.1, under [æ]). In 'r-less' dialects many speakers have a similar nucleus in *scarce, scared, scares, scare,* with or without additional tension at the end of the centering glide. In 'r-pronouncing' dialects the further tension is retracted--[ɛ^ə̭ə̭˞].

For some speakers the item *baa* has [æə̭ˇ]. Such a nucleus is also found for many speakers in *bad, pan, pass, jazz*. In Eastern New England it is also heard in *part, card, barn, bars, harsh,* sometimes with additional tension and centering--[æə̭ˇə̭]. In Western New England speech we find [æə̭ˇə̭˞].

In items like *hurt, heard, burn, nurse, furs, fur* the Eastern and Southern dialects ('r-less' or not) have nuclei like [ɜ^ə̭] or [ɨ^ɨ̽ˇ] (the latter in New England).

In *part, card, barn, bars, harsh* many American and most British speakers have nuclei of the type of [aə̽ˇ], with the first element ranging from [a>] to [ɑ]. Such nuclei (without additional tension or retraction) are also found in *palm, spa*.

In *boor, assured, boors, Bourse,* most speakers other than Northern Middle Western and Far Western have nuclei of the type of [ʊ^ɨ̽ˇ], before the final tension or retraction.

In *bought, daub, dawn, boss, cause, law* many Eastern American speakers and most British speakers use nuclei beginning in [ɔ] or [Ω] (usually fairly tense and well-rounded) and ending in [ə̽]. Such speakers also have the same or similar nuclei in *fort, ford, born, force, pours, wore,* with additional tension or retraction.

Other speakers (Middle and Far Western American, and elsewhere) use, in *bought*, etc., nuclei of the type of [ωə̭˅] or [ɒə̭˅]. In items with *r* some of these speakers use [Ωə̭] in all cases, while others have [Ωə̭] in some and [ω̂ə˅] in others--*hoarse* as against *horse*, *wore* and *war*, *mourning* and *morning*, and so on.

The items in this section all show glides to [ɨ̭˅], [ə̭], or [ə̭˅], starting from positions in the ranges already described before.

1.31. In 1.1 there was presented the evidence for the simple vocalic nuclei of English. It was found that these fall into nine ranges of quality, approximately [I E æ ɨ ʌ< a< U Ω< ɒ]. There were four recognizable degrees of length, e.g., [I: I· Iˢ I]. There were nasalized varieties, as [Į· Ę·], etc.

The criteria for classifying sounds as allophones of the same phoneme may be summarized thus: the sounds should be phonetically similar, they should be in complementary distribution, and they should exhibit pattern congruity with other groups of sounds.

Within each of the nine quality ranges there is a high degree of phonetic similarity. The length differences are in complementary distribution: longest before voiced spirant, rather long before voiced stop and nasal, somewhat long before voiceless spirant, short before voiceless stop; not all dialects have the same distribution, but all have similar patterns; and there are further noticeable variations in length in polysyllabic items. As for nasalization, it is found before and often after nasal consonants, and not elsewhere. Each set of sounds in one quality shows pattern congruity with the others--nasalization in the same situations, and the same conditioning factors for length differences.

The qualities themselves, however, are in contrast: *gist, jest, just* with [ɨ] (adverb), *just* with [ʌ<] (adjective); *put, pot, pat; hull, whole* with [Ω<], (*alco*)*hol* with [ɒ]. Any one of these substituted in any item for one of the others produces another item--whether this be a morpheme of the language or a nonsense-utterance.

There must be, therefore, nine simple vowel phonemes in English as a whole. These are, using the typographically simplest symbols: /i e æ ɨ ə a u o ɔ/; for purposes of easy reference, it is suggested that they be named, respectively, 'eye', 'ee', 'digraph', 'barred eye', 'shwa', 'ai' (as in *paid*), 'you', 'ow' (as in *own*), 'open ow'. They may be referred to as the 'simple' or 'basic' or 'short' vowels of the language.

1.32. In examining other than the simple vocalic nuclei of syllables, we found, in 1.21, 1.22, 1.23, that there were complex nuclei beginning with one of the nine vowel qualities, and ending with offglides of three kinds: a glide to a higher and fronter position--[i̯ ɪ̯ e̯]; one to a higher, back, more rounded position--[u̯ ʊ̯ o̯]; and one to a more central, unrounded position--[ɨ̯ˇ ə̯ ə̯ˇ].

Within each of these three contrasting sets, there is complementary distribution, and the three show pattern congruity with each other: highest allophones after high vowels, lowest after low vowels, intermediate after mid vowels. If each complex is to be taken as a unit, there must be 27 phonemes involved. But the beginnings of the complex nuclei are clearly like allophones of the nine already identified phonemes /i e æ ɨ ə a u o ɔ/, and the ends of them show patterns and distributions expected of separate phonemes. The conclusion is inescapable that the complex nuclei consist each of two phonemes, one of the short vowels followed by one of three glides. Let us designate the glides as /F B C/ for the present; using /V/ as the symbol for any short vowel, the complex nuclei are all /VF VB VC/.

For the further identification of the glides as phonemes it is necessary to consider some additional phonetic data. In the items *yield, you, yore, yet, yoke, yap, yacht,* the initial sound is a palatal onglide with front vowel timbre: *yield, you* have [i̯^], *yet, yoke* have [ɪ̯^], *yap, yacht* have [e̯^]. In *'yit'* for *yet* we find [i̯^] before /ɨ/, in *'yup'* meaning 'yes' we have [I̯^] before /ə/, in *y'all* 'you all', we have [e̯^] before /ɔ/. The height of the onglide is distributed so that the highest forms are before high vowels, the lowest before low vowels, the intermediate before mid vowels. This onglide has generally been considered as a phoneme, /y/, and the allophones here identified satisfy the pertinent criteria.

In the items *we, woo, wet, woe, wagon, watt* we find an onglide that is rounded, with back vowel timbre: [u̯^] in *we, woo,* [U̯^] in *wet, woe,* [o̯^] in *wagon, watt.* Items with /ɨ/ will have [u̯^], those with /ə/ will have [U̯^], those with /ɔ/ will have [o̯^]. The distribution of allophones is exactly parallel to that of those we have put into the phoneme /y/. So we have here a phoneme, /w/, which exhibits pattern congruity with /y/.

In the items *he, hit, hay, help, hat,* or *who, hood, hoe, home* (with /om/), *(alco)hol* (with /ɔl/), or *hut, hot,* the initial sound in each case is made by means of a movement from a more central and less rounded position than that of the following vowel, with voiceless onset, friction noise, and an out-from-the-center glide to the vowel position; the sounds could be symbolized by starting with the following vowel symbols, respectively, [ɨ ɨˇ ə ə əˇ], [ɨ₍w₎ ɨˇ₍w₎ ə₍w₎ ə₍w₎ əˇ₍w₎], [ə əˇ], and adding to each symbol [̯] under it for nonsyllabicity, [‸] under it for voicelessness, and [₊] after it for friction noise. All these sounds are in complementary distribution, their height and rounding being determined by the following vowel; they belong to what is usually called the phoneme /h/.

The allophones of the prevocalic phonemes /y w h/ parallel in quality and distribution those of the post-vocalic glides /F B C/: [i̯^ I̯^ e̯^] and [i̯ I̯ e̯], [u̯^ U̯^ o̯^] and [u̯ U̯ o̯], [ɨ̯ˇ o̯ o̯ˇ] and [ɨ̯ˇ ə̯ əˇ]; in the case of /y w/ the allophones are each a little higher than the corresponding ones of /F/ and /B/, and the highest often have some friction noise. For /h/, the allophones are partly voiceless and have friction-noise onset, while those of /C/ are usually fully voiced, and even when ending voiceless (in utterance-final, for some speakers) are frictionless. There is thus phonetic similarity, the allophones of /y w h/ being onglide mirror-images of the offglides /F B C/. In addition, /y w h/ are in complementary distribution with /F B C/. Finally, the two sets show exact pattern congruity in all their allophones--highest position before or after /i ɨ u/, lowest before or after /æ a ɔ/, intermediate before or after /e ə o/. There is thus no doubt that the only possible PHONEMIC analysis is to put /F B C/ into the phonemes /y w h/ respectively.

The complex nuclei are then to be analyzed as VS/, where /S/ is to be read 'semivowel', defined as one of the three phonemes /y w h/. The term 'semivowel' is, of course, only a label for a class of consonants with certain features in common. In their behavior in initial clusters with other consonants, /y w h/ show no particular symmetry, a fact easily accounted for historically.

1.33. The 36 syllabic nuclei that have been established--nine simple and 27 of the type /VS/, do not, of course, ALL occur in the speech of any one speaker. It is interesting, though, how many are actually so found, the usual situation being five or six simple vowels, and some ten or a dozen vowel-semivowel sequences appearing very frequently, and the other simple vowels and some half a dozen or more complex nuclei being found only in a few, or sometimes even only one, lexical item. An unprejudiced inspection of English speech, however, shows that the overall analysis is necessary for any one speaker because of the distribution of the various items. To facilitate comprehension of the situation, we shall give some examples, for individuals, and for better-known dialects.

The first author of this paper (GLT) has /i e æ ə a u/ occurring with great frequency, in such expected items as *pit, pet, pat, putt, pot, put* respectively. In the adverb *just* he has /ə/ about 25% of the time, especially in formal style, and /ɨ/ the rest of the time; /ɨ/ also occurs regularly in *twenty*, with occasional replacement by /e/;

the item *willies* in 'it gives me the willies' has /ɨ/, contrasting with /i/ in *Willie's* and /u/ in *woolies; until* has /ɨ/ in the second syllable, as has its equivalent *till*, but *till* n. 'a place to keep money' or the verb *till* have /i/; there are also a few other occurrences of /ɨ/, such as *this* part of the time. In the items *boss* 'hump' and *gloss* 'translation', he has /ɔ/ (but *boss* 'superior' and *gloss* 'shine' have /oh/. In *the whole thing, I'm going home* he has /o/ in *whole* most of the time and in *home* about one-fourth of the time. In *bee, bay, buy, boy* GLT has his four regularly occurring /Vy/ sequences--/iy ey ay oy/. Rarely, and only in recent years after living in various parts of the South, he may use /æy/ in *time* or a similar item. In his original northern New Jersey speech there were many instances of /ɨy/, instead of /iy/, surviving now only occasionally in such cases as 'Who--me?', 'See?'. The sequence /əy/ has always been known to him as 'New Yorkese' or 'Brooklynese' in *bird, first,* but has never been used except in facetious imitation of that dialect. The sequences /uy/ and /ɔy/ do not occur in his normal speech. In *do, go, now* GLT has /uw ow æw/, his three frequent /Vw/ sequences; originally many or maybe even most /ow/ items had /əw/, but now /əw/ occurs only occasionally, as in 'Go!', 'So!'. In *now*, etc., /æw/ is often replaced by /aw/, especially in formal style. The sequence /ɨw/ occasionally appears instead of /uw/, especially in formal style in items like *due, Tuesday, sue*. The sequences /iw ew ɔw/ do not normally occur. In *yeah, pa, law* are found GLT's most frequent /Vh/ sequences--/eh ah oh/; /eh/ is frequent because it occurs in *bad, grab, bag, lamb, land, lass, laugh,* etc., where others have /æ/ or /æh/ in some or all of the items; /ah/ is found in *palm, father.* Before *r* the three are also found, as in *dare, bar, door* respectively. Before *r* are also found /ih/ as in *dear*, /əh/ as in *fur*, /uh/ as in *poor*; /ih/ also occurs in *idea, theater*. In *baa* 'cry of a sheep' /æh/ is found. The sequences /ɨh ɔh/ do not normally occur. In imitations of r-less speech, /ih eh ah əh uh oh/ are very frequent. Before *r* and a voiceless consonant (see below, 1.4, 1.5) GLT uses simple /V/ more frequently than /Vh/, as in *fierce, scarce, hurt, part, Newark* = /núrk/ (see below, 1.6 for stress), *port*. In *hurry* GLT has /ə/, but the allophone may or may not have retraction; in *furry*, he has /əh/, with marked terminal retraction; *jury, bureau, Europe* have /u/ rather than /uh/; *merry, marry, Mary* have /e æ eh/ respectively; *here, there* often have /i/ and /e/ instead of /ih/ and /eh/.

The second author's speech (HLS) is very similar structurally to GLT's, with some clear regional differences, especially in allophonic details (he is from Baltimore); both are examples of Central Atlantic Seaboard American English. The items *pit, pet, pat, putt, pot, put* have /i e æ ə a u/; /a/ is central [a] rather than back [ɑ], the central or even fronted central quality being particularly noticeable in such items as *chocolate* and *office* (GLT has /oh/ in both of these). *Just* (adv.) has /e/ (a Southern trait) about 50% of the time, /ə/ about 10% of the time (with a connotation of formal style), and /ɨ/ the rest of the time. In *children* he has /ɨ/ more than half the time, /i/ being formal in this item. The phonetic difference between /i/ and /ɨ/ is greater in this near-Southern than it is further north. The vowel /ɔ/ occurs most of the time in *alcohol*, and in /ɔh/ in such items as *father, palm, part, park*, though the latter now more often have /ah/, with a retracted allophone of the vowel, [ɑ], whereas the more northern /ah/ often has a central vowel, [a]. In *gonna* HLS has /o/. The items *bee, bay, buy, boy* are the same as in GLT's speech; but GLT's /ay/ usually has a back allophone of /a/, whereas HLS has a fronted central variety, with /æy/ appearing occasionally in *I* and *July*. HLS has /uw ow æw/ in *do, go, now*, with /aw/ as a formal style substitute for /æw/, and /əw/ in *house* and *out* still retained from time to time (the vowel being [ə<̬], not [ʌ<]). HLS does not use /əw/ where others have /ow/, nor does he have /ɨw/. The sequences /iw ew ɔw/ don't occur in his speech. In *can* 'am able', *have, has, had, slam, biff-bam, lad*, and before /š/, as in *cash*, HLS has /æ/; /æh/ occurs in *salve*; /eh/ is found otherwise before nasals, voiced stops, and voiceless spirants, as in *can* 'tin container', *bad, path*, etc. Before *r* final or followed by a consonant, HLS regularly has /Vh/ in all items, but occasionally in rapid speech he has *here* and *there* with /i/ and /e/, respectively, and /V/ alone when a voiceless stop follows *r* (*port*). In *hurry, flurry, courage* he has /ə/ without retraction, and *furry* has either /ə/ or /əh/ (the latter with retraction); *merry, marry, Mary* have /e æ eh/ respectively.

In Northern Middle Western the items *pit, pet, cut, put* regularly have /i e ə u/; *cat* and *cot* may have /æ/ and /a/, but for many speakers there is regular or occasional use of /eh/ and /ah/ in such items; /eh/ and /ah/ frequently occur before voiced consonants, as in *bad, odd*. Such items as *log* and *fog* often have /ɔh/ (or even /oh/). In *bee, bay, buy, boy* are found the expected /iy ey ay oy/, and *do, go, now* have /uw ow aw/. In *law*, etc., one finds /ɔh/ more frequently than /oh/. Before *r* there are many speakers who use /V/ regularly, and /Vh/ rarely or never. Many such speakers have /e/ in all three of the items *merry, marry, Mary*; some have /eh/ in all three, while still others have /e/ or /eh/ in *merry, Mary*, and /æ/ in *marry*. The speakers who distinguish *hoarse* from *horse* use /o/ and /ɔ/ or /oh/ and /ɔh/. Occurrences of /ɨ/ and /o/ as simple nuclei are found here and there, and /ɔ/ is common in such items as *sorry, wash*.

In the Southeast of the United States, in both the Coastal and Piedmont speech, are found speakers who use /æy/ in *land, half, pass*. In these regions *law, all*, etc., usually have /ɔw/, while *palm* may have /ɔh/. In *sister, dinner, milk* one often finds /ɨ/, which also occurs in *whip, took* and elsewhere. The adverb *just* may have /e/, and *milk* appears with /e/ also. Some Southern speakers have /eh/ in both *dear* and *dare*, etc. In Southern Coastal one finds /eh/ for /ey/ in such items as *great, afraid*, and /oh/ for /ow/ in *boat, road*, with /əy/ in *bird, first*.

Beginning at Philadelphia and running west and southwest there is a central band, growing broader as it goes west, with sets of characteristics distinguishing it from regions both north and south of it. Philadelphia has /ə/

in *merry, terrible*, many instances of /ɨ/, /ɨy/, /ɨw/ instead of /i/, /iy/, /uw/ and a distribution of /æ æh eh/ that is different from the Central Atlantic seaboard north and south of it. At the headwaters of the Ohio begins the incidence of /æy/ in *ash*, with fewer speakers having also /ɔy/ in *wash*, and a few with /uy/ in *push*.

In older generation standard and present-day substandard New York City speech /əy/ is found in items like *bird, first*. In *park, card, palm* one finds many speakers using /ɔh/ instead of /ah/ (often without following retraction). In *bad, pass*, etc., the nucleus is generally /eh/, though /æh/ or even /æ/ may occur as a conscious substitution by educated speakers. Substandard speakers have allophones with higher initial position, more tension, and some nasal resonance, about [ẹ̃ːə̃̂], as compared with standard [ɛ·ə̂]. Similarly, in *law, loss* one often finds an over-rounded tense, overlong nucleus, [ọ̃ːə̃̂].

In Eastern New England /i e u/ are found in *pit, pet, put*, but such items as *cut* have /a/ (in a centered allophone, about [a˃]), and *cot*, etc., have /ɔ/. In *home, coat, road, whole*, and many other specific items one finds /o/ (the so-called 'New England short o'). Items like *park, cart, card* have /æh/ rather than /ah/, and /æh/ is also found in *pass, dance*, and the like; but *land, bad*, etc., have /æ/ or /eh/. In *bird, first*, etc., is found /ɨh/, with a very tense substandard allophone in Providence and Boston.

The Southern British simple vowel patterning in *cut* and *cot* is like that of Eastern New England, with /ɔ/ having a phonetically higher and tenser variety, [ω]. The adjective *just* has /a/, but the adverb has /ə/; *sum* has /a/, but *some* has /ə/; and there are other such contrasts. Some British speakers use /əw/ or even /ew/ instead of /ow/ in such items as *go, no, oh*, etc. In Cockney and in North of England dialects /ɨ/ and /ɨy/ appear frequently for standard /i/ and /iy/; Cockney speakers have /æy/ for standard /ey/.

The occasional spellings used by dialect writers are often instructive of the distribution of the less usual nuclei presented in this analysis. The example of *mither, ither* for *mother, other*, where /ɨ/ instead of /ə/ is meant, will have to suffice.

We conclude this section with two tables accompanied by notes, which will summarize the occurrence of vocalic nuclei in the several varieties of English.

Table I

	V	*Vy*	*Vw*	*Vh*
/i/	*pit*	*bee*	*few* (11)	*dear* (18)
/e/	*pet*	*bay*	*house* (12)	*dare, yeah*
/æ/	*pat*	*pass* (6)	*house* (13)	*baa*
/ɨ/	*just* (1)	*bee* (7)	*moon* (14)	*fur* (19)
/ə/	*cut* (2)	*bird* (8)	*go* (15)	*fur*
/a/	*cot* (3)	*buy*	*house* (16)	*far, palm*
/u/	*put*	*buoy* (9)	*do*	*boor*
/o/	*home* (4)	*boy*	*go*	*pour, paw*
/ɔ/	*wash* (5)	*wash* (10)	*law* (17)	*war* (20), *paw* (21)

(1) The adverb; in Southern British it has /ə/.
(2) Southern British and Coastal New England have /a/.
(3) Southern British and Coastal New England have /ɔ/.
(4) Coastal New England.
(5) Southern British, Coastal New England, and Northern Middle Western.
(6) Southeastern U.S.
(7) Philadelphia, Cockney.
(8) New York City, Southern Coastal
(9) When in one syllable; some speakers have /uy/ in *push*, etc.
(10) Speakers who have /uy/ in *push* will have /ɔy/ in *wash* and /æy/ in *ash*; /ɔy/ in *wash* will occur without /uy/ in *push*.
(11) Old-fashioned, instead of /yuw/.
(12) Tidewater Virginia, allophonically [ᴇᴜ̯˔].

(13) Very widespread in Eastern and Southern U.S.
(14) From Philadelphia west and southwest in a narrow band, allophonically [ɨu̯̇] or [ʊ̇u̯̇].
(15) Southern British and elsewhere.
(16) Southern British, Middle Western American.
(17) Southeastern U.S.
(18) All the items with *r* in this column have /Vh/ in the 'r-less' dialects.
(19) In Eastern New England.
(20) Where distinguished from *wore* with /oh/.
(21) Northern Middle Western.

Table II.

	VrV	*VrC* (7)	*Vhr* (11)	*VhrV* (11)
/i/	*spirit*	*dear*	*dear*	*dearer* (15)
/e/	*merry*	*dare*	*dare*	*Mary* (16)
/æ/	*marry*	*dare* (8)	*dare* (12)	(11)
/ɨ/	*furry* (1)	*fur* (9)	*fur* (13)	(12)
/ə/	*hurry* (2)	*fur*	*fur*	*furry* (17)
/a/	*sorry* (3)	*far*	*far*	*starry* (18)
/u/	*jury* (4)	*boor*	*boor*	*boorish* (19)
/o/	*story* (5)	*hoarse*	*wore*	*pouring* (20)
/ɔ/	*sorry* (6)	*horse* (10)	*war* (14)	*warring* (21)

(1) Where different from *hurry* in quality but not in length.
(2) The allophone may be non-retracted and quite like other allophones of /ə/, or it may be more central and have considerable retraction.
(3) Different from *starry* in length.
(4) Different from *boorish*.
(5) Different from *pouring*.
(6) Speakers who have /ɔ/ in *sorry* may have simple /a/ in *starry*.
(7) Most Northern Middle Western speakers have simple vowel before final or preconsonantal *r*, and the examples in this column are for such speakers. In other

regions there are specific lexical items that have or may have simple nuclei in this situation, as /ir/ in *here*, /er/ in *there*, unstressed *for* with /ər/, unstressed /ar/ in *our*, and /ur/ in *Newark*.

(8) Some Southern Middle Western speakers have /æ/ in *dare;* the dialect-story spelling *b'ar* for *bear* refers to this. In Western New England /æ/ may appear in *bar* instead of /a/.

(9) Where *furry* has /ɨ/, *fur* usually also does.

(10) Where *hoarse* and *horse* are not alike, the latter has /ɔ/.

(11) See note 7. These columns exemplify other than Northern Middle Western dialects.

(12) See note 8.

(13) See note 9.

(14) A difference parallel to that noted in (10).

(15) Different from *mirror* with /i/.

(16) Different from *merry* with /e/ and *marry* with /æ/. Eastern and Southern American, and Southern British speakers distinguish all three of these items. In Philadelphia and vicinity *merry* has /ə/. Some Middle Western speakers distinguish *marry* with /æ/ from the other two both with /e/ or /eh/ (the decision as to whether /h/ is present or not depending on the total structure of the dialect).

(17) Where *fur* has a complex nucleus.

(18) See notes 3 and 6.

(19) See note 4.

(20) See note 5.

(21) See notes 10 and 14.

The syllabic nuclei discussed so far have been shown in stressed syllables. The discussion of the nuclei occurring in the weakest syllables is postponed until the several stress phonemes have been established--1.61, 1.63.

1.4. In initial position in an utterance the following simple consonantal sounds occur in English: [p‘ t‘ k‘ ^{p}b ^{t}d ^{k}g f θ s š ^{f}v $^{\theta}$ð ^{s}z m n l ɹ ʔ]--as in, respectively, *pick, tick, kick, big, dig, gig, fin, thin, sin, shin, vain, then, zone, me, knee, low, row, oh.* The aspiration of [p' t' k'] is found to vary from very slight to rather heavy, these stops being quite fortis. In [ᵇ̥b ᵈ̥d ᵍ̥g] the voiceless onset is always quite marked, and for some speakers there is very little voicing; these stops are lenis. In both [k'] and [ᵍ̥g] there is fronting before a high front vowel, as in *kid, key,* and backing before a high back vowel, as in *cook, cool,* while a central position is found elsewhere, as in *kept, cat, cut, cot, comb;* some Southeastern U.S. speakers have fronted [k̂ ĝ] in such items as *cart, garden* ("kyart", "gyarden"), though more speakers seem to have /y/ after [k̂] and [ĝ]. The symbol [š] can serve as a cover for the several types of groove spirants occurring, as in *shoe*--prepalatal [ś], midpalatal [š], cacuminal [ṣ]. The voiced spirants have even more marked voiceless onset than the voiced stops, but develop a full voicing at the end of the articulation. A voiced spirant with similar onset, [ᶻ̥̌ž], occurs with some speakers rarely, not at all with others. Many speakers do not have [ᶞ̥ð], but use instead an affricate [ᵈ̥ð], or even a dental stop, [ᵈ̥d̪], quite different from [ᵈ̥d]. The sounds [m n l ɹ] are quite short. The position of [t' ᵈ̥d n l] is alveolar generally, though in Scotland a dental position is heard (and in the United States there are native speakers, both with and without a foreign language background, who use dentals). The [l] is generally velarized [lₓ] in the United States, except in the Southeast where, as in Southern England, it is neutral or fronted in timbre--[lₔ] or [lᵢ]; some speakers have a velar lateral, [ʟ]. The [ɹ] is a frictionless spirant made by retraction or raising of the front part of the tongue; many speakers have greater or less lip-rounding accompanying it; some speakers have much lip-rounding and very little retraction; still others use a kind of back-tongue spirant, with lip-rounding. The glottal stop [ʔ] may be rather strong in emphatic utterance, but otherwise is weak or absent.

In addition to the above sounds, there are also, of course, the various allophones of the phonemes /y w h/ already established in 1.32.

Complex initial consonant sounds of these types occur: voiceless or voiced stop and non-groove spirants followed by lateral or retracted spirant or palatal or labial offglide; groove spirant followed by stop, nasal, lateral, retracted, and semivowel offglides; and groove spirant plus stop plus lateral, retracted, or semivowel offglide. Illustrations are: *play* [pˡlₓ], *pray* [pᵈɹ], *pure* [pⁱi̯], *pueblo* [pᵁu̯], *try* [tᵈ+ɹ+], *tune* [tⁱi̯] (for some speakers only--others simply have [t‘]), *twinge* [tᵘu̯], *clay* [kˡlₓ], *cry* [kᵈɹ], *cure* [kⁱi̯], *quick* [kᵘu̯], *blow* [ᵇblₓ], *brew* [ᵇbɹ], *beauty* [ᵇbi̯], *dry* [ᵈdɹ+], *due* [ᵈdi̯] (for some speakers--others have [ᵈd]), *dwell* [ᵈdu̯], *glee* [ᵍglₓ], *grey* [ᵍgɹ], *gewgaw* [ᵍgi̯], *Gwynn* [ᵍgu̯], *flee* [fˡlₓ], *free* [fᵈɹ], *few* [fⁱi̯], *three* [θᵈɹ], *thews* [θⁱi̯], *thwack* [θᵒo̯], *hue* [i̯+ⁱi̯], *when* [u̯+ᵁu̯] (for some--others have [u̯]), *chew* [t>ʸš], *jaw* [ᵈd>ʸž], *slay* [sˡlₓ], *sue* [sⁱi̯] (for some--others have [s]), *sway* [sᵁu̯], *spin* [sP], *stand* [sT], *skin* [sK], *sphere* [sf], *svelte* [sᵛv], *smile* [sᵐm], *snow* [sⁿn]; *Schlitz* [šˡlₓ], *shrink* [šᵈɹ], *Schwartz* [šᵁu̯], *shmoo* [šᵐm], *Schneider* [šⁿn] (Southeastern speakers often have [s] instead of [š] in the last five types); *spleen* [sPˡlₓ], *spray* [sPᵈɹ], *spew* [sPⁱi̯], *stray* [sTᵈɹ], *stew* [sTⁱi̯] (for some--others have [sT]), *sclerosis* [sKˡlₓ], *scream* [sKᵈɹ], *skew* [sKⁱi̯], *square* [sKᵁu̯].

In final position in an utterance the following simple consonants occur: [p˥ t˥ k˥ bᵇ dᵈ gᵍ f θ s š vᵛ ðᶞ zᶻ žᶻ m· n· ŋ· lₓ· ə·]--as in *tip, pit, tick, rub, red, rug, rough, myth, miss, push, give, bathe, rose, rouge, dim, din, sing, fill, car.* The voiceless stops may also occur aspirated, [p‘ t‘ k‘], as free alternations (in emphatic speech, usually) for the non-released ones. For the voiced stops the final voicelessness is marked. The spirant [š] is of the same varieties as initially, and the same variation holds for [žᶻ]. The voiced spirants show marked devoicing, especially [zᶻ]. The nasals and lateral and retraction are noticeably long. The retraction varies in extent, for some speakers being quite strong (almost [ɹ]--Northern Middle Western, some northern British), with others being very weak (most 'r-less' dialects).

Final complex consonants are numerous: any voiceless stop or non-groove spirant plus [s] offglide, any voiced stop or non-groove spirant or nasal or lateral or retraction plus [z^{ž}^] offglide--as in *lips, hits, kicks, cliffs, myths, rubs, reds, rugs, gives, bathes, dims, dins, sings, fills, cars;* nasal plus voiceless stop or [d] or a spirant, with or without additional sibilant offglide--as in *limp, hint, land, link, limps, hints, lands, links, fence, Corinth, triumph;* the affricates [t>$_{y}^{\check{s}}$] and [d>$_{y}^{\check{z}}$]--*such, pinch, judge, hinge* (the latter ending voiceless); lateral or retraction plus stop or spirant or both--*fault, faults, force, forced,* etc.

The heaviest combinations of consonant articulations are to be found in such items as *glimpsed* [mpsт˺], *fenced* [ntsт˺] (some speakers only--others have [nsт˺], *jinxed* [ŋksт˺], *worlds* [ɹ̣ɹ̣l$_x$dz^{ž}]; they are few in number, can be easily listed, and simple covering statements can be made about them.

Internally in utterances the consonant sequences and articulations are more varied than the initial or terminal possibilities. We shall indicate only some of the occurrences here, taking up others below in 1.62. The consonants [p‘ t‘ k‘ t>š‘] are found before stressed vowels (see 1.61), and [p k t>š] (fortis unaspirated released) before weak vowels; [b d g d>ž v ð z ž] (fully voiced), and [f θ s š m n˙ l$_x$ ɹ] are found in either situation; [ŋ] is found before weak-stressed vowels; all the possible combinations of two and three consonant articulations are found. Examples of these internal consonants (a sampling only) are: *appear, attack, occur, achieve, apple, pocket, teacher, rubber, ladder, begging, judging, living, wither, roses, vision, bluffing, pithy, missing, pushing, summer, dinner, filling, merry, singer* [ŋ], *finger* [ŋg], *lasting, alter, artist, ample, antler, strengthen* [ŋθ] or [ŋkθ], *glimpsing, nitrate, worldly,* etc., etc. In *butter* we find a voiced fortis [t̬] in most American speech, with [t‘] in Southern British and [t] in some other regions; *hunting* with many speakers has [nɪ], a flap-release short nasal;

button has [ˀₜn̩] or [tn̩]; *mountain* has [nˀn̩] or [ntn̩]; *tle* has [t̬l̩] or [tl̩], and [ˀₜl̩] with some (often substa...-ard) speakers; there are speakers who have [t̬l̩] in *rattle* and [ˀₜl̩] in *prattle*.

1.5. On the basis of the usual criteria of phonemic analysis, the statements for most of the consonant phonemes of English can be easily made from the foregoing phonetic data.

The articulations [pʻ p ᴘ p˥] are in complementary distribution: [pʻ] initial, internal before stressed vowel, final in 'free alternation' with [p˥]; [p] internal before weak vowel, everywhere before [ˡ̂l ˆɹ] and other consonants; [ᴘ] after [s]; [p˥] final. Other similar articulations, in various combinations of consonant sounds, are also in complementary distribution with those just listed. It is easy to construct a phoneme /p/ from these data. The only possible doubt is in regard to [ᴘ], which bears phonetic similarity to [ᵇ̂b b bᵇ̂] also and is in complementary distribution with them as well as with [pʻ p p˥]. An examination of patterned sequences like [sᴘ], [sᴛ], [sᴋ] and [zb] (*asbestos*), [zdᵈ̂] (*raised*) indicates that after [s] there is /p/ not /b/, /t/ not /d/, /k/ not /g/ (see further for these phonemes other than /p/).

The phoneme /k/ is in like manner composed of [kʻ k ᴋ k˥] and similar sounds.

The sounds [tʻ t t̬ ᴛ t˥] make up a phoneme /t/ in a similar way. For speakers who have sounds like [ˀₜ], these are also usually easily assignable to the /t/ phoneme. The situation where *rattle* has [t̬] and *prattle* has [ˀₜ] is seen to be a complex case of complementary distribution: [t̬] occurs after one of the short vowel phonemes, before [l̩], when the vowel is preceded by one consonant, as in *bottle, rattle*, or by /s/ plus consonant, as in *spittle, scuttle*; [ˀₜ] occurs before [l̩] after a vowel when the vowel is preceded by a consonant cluster, as in *prattle, Brattleboro, brittle*; after a /VS/ sequence, [t̬] or [t] and [ˀₜ] are in free alternation before [l̩]. In *mountain*, etc., the [ˀ] is an interruption in the voicing of a continuously held [n]-position; in *hunting* the flap effect of the $[n^{1}]$ is a not dissimilar denasalization; these sounds are for most speakers in free alternation with [t], and are in contrast with allophones of /p/ or /k/--*dumpin'* (for *dumping*), *Lincoln*--and with the possible vowel-onset [$^{?}$] as in *drown in*... . Including these sounds in the phoneme /t/ is thus seen to be a difficulty merely of complete and unambiguous statement.

The phonemes /b d g/ are constituted by the congruently patterned sets of allophones $[{}^{b}_{\wedge}b\ b\ b^{b}_{\wedge}]$, $[{}^{d}_{\wedge}d\ d\ d^{d}_{\wedge}]$, $[{}^{g}_{\wedge}g\ g\ g^{g}_{\wedge}]$.

The sequence $[t{>}_{y}{}^{\check{s}}]$, with and without aspiration, is to be analyzed as a unit phoneme, there being contrasts like *scorching* with $[t{>}^{\check{s}}]$ and *courtship* with [tš](see 1.62 for the similar but not identical sequence in *sport-shoe*); we shall use /c/ as the symbol for this phoneme. Some speakers, however, do have here a sequence /tš/; others may possibly have /ty/. If /c/ is a unit, then /j/ must be constituted as a unit composed of the varieties of $[d{>}_{y}{}^{\check{z}}]$.

The phonemes /f θ s š/ have one allophone each.

The phonemes /v ð z ž/ have the patterned sets of allophones $[{}^{v}_{\wedge}v\ v\ v^{v}_{\wedge}]$, etc.

The phonemes /m n/ have the allophones [m m·] and [n n·]; the flapped nasal $[n^{1}]$ is in contrast with internal [n], and is analyzed as /nt/--*running* with /n/, *hunting* with /nt/.

The sounds [ŋ ŋ·] constitute the phoneme /ŋ/, not occurring initially or before a stressed vowel. There are speakers in some regions of Great Britain and of the Southeast of the United States, as well as some other American speakers in (usually) urban centers where there is a strong background of certain other languages--not necessarily in the speaker's own family history--who do not distinguish *singer* and *finger*, but have a velar nasal with fast denasalization, $[\breve{ŋ}^{g}]$, in both; such speakers have [ŋ] or $[\breve{ŋ}^{g}]$ in final position (*sing*), and [ŋ] before /k/ (*think*); for them [ŋ ŋ̆] are allophones of /n/, and $[^{g}]$ is an allophone of /g/, so that *singer, finger, sing, think* have /ng ng ng nk/ respectively; they have no phoneme /ŋ/.

The phoneme /l/ has allophones [l_x] and [l]; some speakers (GLT, HLS) have [l] only before /y/, as in *William, million*; others have [l] also before vowels; still others rarely have [l] at all; the amount of velarization of [l_x] varies widely.

The sounds [ɹ ^ɹ ɹ+ ^ɹ+] are allophones of a phoneme /r/. With them must be put the retraction [ɚ̽] that occurs after vocalic nuclei; in most of the so-called 'r-less' dialects there is enough additional phonetic material after the centering offglide to constitute an allophone of /r/; the postvocalic allophones of /r/, then, vary widely, as do the prevocalic ones.

The phonemes /w y h/ have already been discussed.

The consonant phonemes of English are then the following: /p t k b d g c j f θ s š v ð z ž m n ŋ l r w y h/

The initial clusters that occur are: /pl pr py pw tr tw kl kr ky kw bl br by dr dw gl gr gy gw fl fr fy θr θy θw hy hw vy my sl sw sp st sk sf sv sm sn šl šr šw šn spl spr spy str skl skr sky skw/, and /ty dy sy zy sty/ for some speakers; some also have /ts/.

Final clusters may be illustrated by a partial list: /ps ts ks fs θs bz dz gz vz ðz mz nz ŋz lz rz ns ls rs mp nt nd ŋk mps nts ndz ŋks nθ mf nc nj lp lt lk lps rst/, etc. The heaviest clusters mentioned in 1.4 are /mpst/, /ntst/ (for some speakers only), /ŋkst/, /hrldz/.

1.61. English utterances containing more than one vowel exhibit marked differences in loudness, concentrated on the vowels. These different loudnesses are found to be consistent in their RELATIVE strengths, and their location is seen to be constant within systematic possibilities of variation. The presumption is that they are indications or results of the presence of phonemic entities. Utterances having only one vowel are found to be said always with a loudness equal to the greatest loudness found in larger utterances--under the same conditions of style, emphasis, and so on. This indicates that the functioning of the degrees of loudness is limited, but essentially this limitation is no different from the limitations found for vowels and consonants, for example: only /ə/ as a final vowel in most English dialects; only the stated clusters of consonants, and so on.

The degree of loudness heard in the monosyllables *yes, go,* in the first syllable of *under, going,* and in the second syllable of *above, allow,* may be used as a standard of measurement for other stresses. From the disyllabic examples it is apparent that loud stress, [ˈ], and soft stress, [˘], are two different entities; some would prefer to say that the non-loud syllables under discussion have no stress, but since we are talking at this stage about hearable things, it seems better to have a positive rather than a negative terminology. On the basis of the data so far, there must be a stress phoneme whose characteristic is maximum normal loudness, which we may call PRIMARY STRESS and indicate as /´/, putting the accent mark over the vowel: /yés gów ə́ndər gówiŋ əbə́v əlǽw/ (for the vocalic nuclei of the syllables used in illustrations in this section which are not under primary stress see 1.63).

Do the instances of [˘] constitute a phoneme, or are they merely indications of the absence of [´]? Let us examine trisyllabic items like *animal, terrific.* In *animal* there is [´] on the first syllable; the last two syllables are soft stressed, but the last is a bit stronger than the middle one, say [˘] and [˘̲]. In *terrific* the primary is on the middle syllable and the first and last syllables are about equally [˘]. Since it is precisely degree of loudness that we are examining, it cannot be said that these differing softer loudnesses are merely characteristics of the vowels of syllables without /´/. They must be allophones of a phoneme of loudness, in this case a WEAK stress, /˘/; we have then /ǽnɨ̆mə̆l tɨ̆rífɨ̆k/.

In items like *animate* (verb), *refugee* (with primary on the first syllable), it is found that the last vowel is louder than the instances of /˘/ examined above, say [˘̲].

In *animate* the nucleus bearing [=̆] is /ey/, while in *animal* or *animate* (adjective) the last nucleus is /ɨ/ (or /ə/); it might be argued that the extra loudness is allophonic in relation to the different nucleus. But in *refugee* the final nucleus is /iy/ just as it is in *effigy*, and the difference in stress is still there. So [=̆] is in phonemic contrast with [-̆], and must then be set up as a phoneme, which we may call TERTIARY stress, written /`/, (see 1.62 for the term SECONDARY STRESS). The examples cited are: /ǽnɨ̌mèyt réfyŭjìy éfɨ̌jǐy/. Once again remembering that we are dealing with degrees of loudness, we conclude that wherever there is [=̆] it constitutes an allophone of the phoneme /`/, whether or not there is direct minimal contrast with /˘/. So we have *sýntàx, cóntènts, ànĭmátiŏn, hètĕrŏgénĕŏus, díctiŏnàry̆*, etc. After this analysis is made it becomes clear that in English only one weak syllable may precede a primary at the beginning of utterance. After a primary or other strong stress, the most common patterns have one or two weaks, but **there** are instances of three, and even four: *úndĕr, ánĭmăl, práctĭcăblĕ, práctĭcăblĕnĕss.*

There are then three stress phonemes to be found in items of one, two, three or more syllables of the kind illustrated: primary, tertiary, weak--/´`˘/. Except where a positive symbolization is required, weak stress may be left unmarked.

In the next section it will be seen that there is still another stress phoneme--secondary, /ˆ/.

1.62. In univocalic items (exhibiting only primary stress) the phonetic characteristics of the manner of offglide and onset from any one segmental phoneme to the next (note that this excludes the beginning of the initial phoneme and the end of the final phoneme) are taken to be the manner of normal transition from one phoneme to another. This is symbolized by writing the vowel and consonant symbols without a space between them: /yúw stréŋθ lúkt/. When an explicit symbol is needed, the tie-line (‿) may be used --but it is not a phoneme symbol.

In plurivocalic items such as those mentioned in 1.61, the same kind of normal transition is found. But there are other plurivocalic items which exhibit different transitions. In comparing *nitrate* with *night-rate* we find the same segmental phonemes and the same stresses, but the manner of transition from /t/ to /r/ is different. The first item has normal transition, the second, being in direct contrast with it, must be phonemically different--must have, that is, some additional phoneme present. This additional feature, phonetically the manner in which one ends the /t/ and goes on to the /r/, is set up as an instance of internal open juncture, symbolized by /+/ (hence, 'plus-juncture'). The two items cited are then: /náytrèyt/ and /náyt+rèyt/.

Similar interrupted transitions are to be found in the following instances, each compared with a minimally differing item having normal transition or the interruption at a different point: *slyness* /sláy+nɨs/: *minus* /máynɨs/; *in the ...* /în+ðə/ as said with separation of the items compared with /inðə/ = [ɪn̆ð̬ə]; *is the ...* /iz+ðə/: /izðə/ = [ɪzz̬ə]; *all the ...* /òhl+ðə/: /òhlðə/ with [l$_x$l̥^+_x]; *ice cream* /àys+kríym/ (also /áys+krìym/): *I scream* /ày+skríym/; *School today* /skúwl+.../: *'S cool today* /s+kúwl+.../; *an aim* /ən+éym/: *a name* /ə+néym/ or /ənéym/. The occurrence of plus juncture varies as do the occurrences of other phonemes, regionally and individually. Any one of the cited instances may not occur in a speaker's usage, but he will have others. Thus some say *Plato* as /pléytòw/ (or /..tŏw/), with [t̬] for /t/, while others will say /pléy+tòw/, with a longer /ey/ and [tʻ] for /t/.

A full study of the phonetic characteristics of phonemes before /+/ has not yet been made. Generally speaking, the /VS/ sequences and the consonants appear as they do when final in an utterance. Consideration of this matter clarifies and extends the description of the allophones of the segmental phonemes in normal transition. Thus, the special allophones in /nð zð lð/ are likely to be noted and identified only after /+/ has been set up and one has noted the characteristics of /n+ð z+ð l+ð/.

Once the structure point symbolized by /+/ has been established, further examination leads to the identification of additional facts about stress. Items like *elevator, operator, operation* are describable in terms of the stress levels /´`˘/ already identified (1.61): /élɨ̆vèytə̆r/, /ápə̆rèytə̆r/, /àpə̆réysə̆n/. When the complex sequence *elevator-operator* is examined, it is clear that the stress on /ap/ is stronger than that on the syllables marked /`/ in the isolated item, say [∸]. It is conceivable, however, that this might be an allophone of /`/; but when we compare *elevator-operator* with *elevator-operation*, it becomes clear that [∸], wherever located, is phonemically different from /`/. Let us call it SECONDARY stress, marking it with /^/; we have these possibilities: *élĕvàtŏr+ôpĕràtŏr* 'person who operates an elevator'; *êlĕvàtŏr+ópĕràtŏr 'id.'* --contrasted with, say, the starter; *élĕvàtŏr+òpĕrâtiŏn* 'the operation of elevators'; *êlĕvàtŏr+òpĕrátiŏn 'id.'*-- contrasted with, say, the repair of elevators. Examples of /^/ are found to be numerous: *òld+máid* 'spinster': *ôld+máid* 'former servant'; *Lòng+Íslănd is a lông+íslănd; bláck+bìrd* but *bláck+bôard* (GLT and HLS); *Whíte+Hòuse* but *(he lives in a) whíte+hôuse (not a brown one)*. A limitation on the occurrence of /^/ is that there are only as many instances of it in an utterance as there are instances of /+/; but there may be more pluses than secondaries, for plus occurs with tertiaries and weaks, as we have seen.

1.63. The vowels occurring in weak-stressed syllables show considerable phonetic differences from those found in syllables with the three strong stresses /´^`/. It has been implied by the treatment above, however, that they are allophones of already established vowel phonemes. There is very considerable variation in usage in many instances, and this has led many investigators to conclusions in which the segmental and stress aspects of the matter, as well as the phonemic and morphophonemic levels, seem confused. We shall attempt to separate out the several levels.

In the first syllables of items like *pituitary, petition, duration, exterior, above, obey, abstract* (vb.),

October, already may be found the following sounds, respectively: [ɪ ɨ ᴜ ᴇ> ə ɷ æ a ω]. In *exterior* many speakers have [ɨ], in *obey* many have [ɷʏ̯], in *already* many have [ɷ] or [ɷə̯]. These are all definitely shorter and less 'clear' than in strong syllables, but there is no difficulty in assigning them phonemically: /i ɨ u/, /e/ or /ɨ/, /ə/, /o/ or /ow/, /æ a/, /ɔ/ or /o/ or /oh/ for the words cited.

In the final syllable of *sofa* we have [ə] for most speakers, [ɨ˅] for some. Whether this latter sound is to be assigned to /ɨ/ or /ə/ depends on the total structure of the dialect, but in most cases assignment would have to be to /ɨ/ on the basis of phonetic similarity. Many speakers have contrasts between *roses* and *Rosa's, I see 'im* and *I see 'em,* with [ɨ˅] in the first of each pair and [ə] in the second; here the phonemic analysis is perfectly clear --/ɨ/ in *roses, 'im,* and /ə/ in *Rosa's, 'em;* other examples are *service* and *serve us, Alice* and *Dallas,* etc. Other speakers do not have contrasts like these, but have [ɨ˅] in some items, often seemingly conditioned by the consonantal surroundings, and [ə] elsewhere, similarly conditioned; nonetheless, the phonemic analysis must assign each instance to either /ɨ/ or /ə/ on the basis of phonetic similarity, since the two exist as separate points of structure elsewhere. The same kind of reasoning applies, of course, to instances of [ɪ] in weak syllables; this is /i/; examples are: *candid*--/i/, *landed*--/ɨ/; *valid*--/i/, *timid*--/ɨ/ or /i/; *crisis*--/i/, *menace*--/ɨ/; etc. It is a phonemic problem to identify the weak vowels in any specific item as /i/ or /ɨ/ or /ə/, or some other; but the statement that different speakers have different vowels in the same item, or that a suffix or the like may have any such vowel indifferently, is outside the level of phonemics. The making of such distributional statements (in terms of class and geographical dialects, and within a dialect in terms of specific morphemes) is a necessary part of the total description of English, but it must be emphasized that the studies leading to such morphophonemic statements can be meaningful only when the phonemic treatment is done rigidly on its own level. The data for this type of study would become available by the gathering of complete morpheme lists.

This is also the place at which to consider the phonemic structure of the final syllables of such words as *bottom, button, bottle, butter.* Phonetically we have what have been described as 'syllabic *m, n, l, r*' that is [ṃ ṇ ḷ ə˞]. But closer inspection makes it clear that there may be different vocalic timbres to the syllabicity, especially for [ṇ] and [ḷ]. In GLT's speech, *button, cushion* have [ṇ] with [ɨ] timbre, while *nation* has [ə] timbre. Similarly, *evil* has [ḷ] with [ɨ] timbre, while *able* has [ḷ] with [ə] timbre. As in the case of other instances of variation between /ɨ/ and /ə/ in the same lexical item or suffix, the speaker uses one or the other, and phonemically there is no problem. For [ṃ] and [ə˞] GLT always has [ə] timbre, but other speakers exhibit the same kind of variation as for [ṇ] and [ḷ]. The phonemic analysis of the 'syllabic liquids and nasals' is, then, either /əm ən əl ər/ or /ɨm ɨn ɨl ɨr/, depending on what the speaker says. It is generally true that the allophones of /ɨ/ are the shortest, in absolute terms, of any vowel; in the 'syllabics' containing /ɨ/, the shortness is very apparent; those with /ə/ are less short. In the same item a speaker may vary from /ɨn/ to /ən/ to /ə̀n/ in adjacent utterances. The remarks above about the distributional statements in regard to weak vowels apply here with equal force.

1.71. The examination of the pitch phenomena of English involves the understanding of the fact that it is relative, not absolute, pitch that is being discussed. Also to be noted is the prelinguistic finding that pitch as used in language is heard around a limited number of points rather than as a continuum.

Extensive testing of spoken English material has convinced us of the correctness of the independent conclusions of Pike and Wells that there are four pitch phonemes in English. Our presentation of the supporting data will be in terms of this conclusion.

The data can be shown in a few typical sentences. Speakers who do not say these as they are shown here can easily supply other examples to replace them. Symbols used to indicate levels of pitch are: [^{1}] for lowest, [^{2}], [^{3}], [^{4}], for successively higher levels; variations within any level are shown by [ˇ] for the lowest, [•] for the next higher variety, [^] for still higher, [-] ('underline') for the highest, as [$\overset{2}{\vee}$ $\overset{2}{\bullet}$ $\overset{2}{\wedge}$ $\underline{2}$]; [¨] means terminal sustention at the level previously marked; [$^+$] means terminal rise from the previously marked level; [$^-$] ('minus') means terminal fall from the previously marked level. The examples are given in ordinary spelling, followed by a PHONEMIC transcription of the vowels, consonants, plus juncture, and stresses, while pitches are shown PHONETICALLY before each syllable.

The first example is the following:

How do they study?

In normal American speech this may be transcribed, as to segmental phonemes, pluses, and stresses, thus:

/hæ̂w+də+ðèy+stə́diy/

When said in this manner, the recognizable pitches are:

(a) /[$\overset{2}{\wedge}$]hæ̂w+[$\overset{2}{\vee}$]də+[$\overset{2}{\bullet}$]ðèy+[$\underline{3}$]stə́[$\overset{1}{\vee}$]diy[$^-$]/.

The pitches marked [$\underline{3}$] and [$\overset{1}{\vee}$] and the terminal fall [$^-$], may be left to one side for a moment. The several [^{2}]s are seen to vary directly with the stress; lower absolute pitch ([$\overset{2}{\vee}$]) on a weak syllable than on a tertiary ([$\overset{2}{\bullet}$]), higher absolute pitch ([$\overset{2}{\wedge}$]) on a secondary than on a tertiary. The pitch associated with the tertiary may be considered as the standard of comparison for each speaker. Without changing the stresses, one may change the pitch distribution to get this:

(b) /[$\overset{3}{\wedge}$]hæ̂w+[$\overset{2}{\vee}$]də+[$\overset{2}{\bullet}$]ðèy+[$\underline{2}$]stə́[$\overset{2}{\vee}$]diy[$^+$]/.

Again leaving aside the [$\overset{3}{\wedge}$], and also the final [$^+$], we see that [$\underline{2}$], an absolutely highest variety of [^{2}], occurs with the primary stress. The change from one to another of these variations of [^{2}] probably occurs at the beginnings of syllables, or, when within a syllable, toward the end of the nucleus, but whatever the exact mechanism (and more research is needed), it may be considered as a phenomenon of normal transition (see below, 1.72, for further discussion of this point). The variations illustrate recognizable allophones of a pitch phoneme symbolized by /^{2}/.

The example just given is usually associated with a British manner of speaking. In American English it is more usual, when putting an occurrence of pitch level [^{3}] at the beginning of the sentence, also to put the primary stress there. When this happens, all the rest of the sentence is usually said on the level of pitch [^{1}], thus:

(c) /[$\overset{3}{-}$]hǽw+[$\overset{1}{\vee}$]də+[$\overset{1}{\bullet}$]ðěy+[$\overset{1}{\wedge}$]stə̂[$\overset{1}{\vee}$]diy[$^{-}$]/.

Still not considering the [$\overset{3}{-}$] and the [$^{-}$], we see that the instances of [^{1}] vary in absolute pitch in the same way as those of [^{2}]. Let us now say *How do they study, then,* thus:

(d) /[$\overset{3}{-}$]hǽw+[$\overset{1}{\vee}$]də+[$\overset{1}{\bullet}$]ðèy+[$\overset{1}{\wedge}$]stə̂[$\overset{1}{\vee}$]diy[$^{-}$][$\overset{1}{-}$]ðén[$^{-}$]/.

We have an instance of an absolutely higher [$\overset{1}{-}$] associated with primary stress on the beginning of /ðén/. The phoneme /^{1}/ has allophones parallel to those of /^{2}/.

We now go back to our first example, and compare it with the others for the absolute pitches of the syllables marked with [^{3}]. In /[$\overset{3}{-}$]stə́/ and /[$\overset{3}{-}$]hǽw/ the pitches are the same, quite high; in /[$\overset{3}{\wedge}$]hæ̂w/, the pitch is a little lower. Suppose now that any of our examples is asked as an echo-question, thus:

(e) /[$\overset{3}{-}$]hǽw+[$\overset{3}{\vee}$]də+[$\overset{3}{\bullet}$]ðèy+[$\overset{3}{\wedge}$]stə̂[$\overset{3}{\vee}$]diy[$^{+}$]/.

Ignoring the terminal [$^{+}$], we have instances of pitches at the [^{3}] level with absolute variations parallel to those of /^{1}/ and /^{2}/; the variations are allophones of the pitch phoneme /^{3}/.

All the examples given so far can now be said over again with a distinctly higher pitch replacing each instance of /^{3}/. We get:

(aa) /...[$\overset{4}{-}$]stə́[$\overset{1}{\vee}$]diy/;

(bb) /[$\overset{4}{\wedge}$]hæ̂w.../;

(cc) /[$\overset{4}{-}$]hǽw.../;

(dd) /[$\overset{4}{-}$]hǽw.../;

(ee) /[$\overset{4}{-}$]hǽw+[$\overset{4}{\vee}$]də+[$\overset{4}{\bullet}$]ðèy+[$\overset{4}{\wedge}$]stə̂[$\overset{4}{\vee}$]diy[$^{+}$]/.

These, then, are allophones of /^{4}/, completely parallel to the other pitches.

1.72. In examples (a), (c), (d) in 1.71 we have instances of a falling pitch [$\overset{1}{\vee}$]...[$^{-}$], and in (d) we have the falling [$\overset{1}{-}$]...[$^{-}$]. In (b) we have [$\overset{2}{\vee}$]...[$^{+}$], and in (e) [$\overset{3}{\vee}$]...[$^{+}$]. In (ee) we have [$\overset{4}{\vee}$]...[$^{+}$]. It might appear that in terminal position the allophone of /^{1}/ drops, while those of /^{2}/, /^{3}/, /^{4}/ rise. The instance of [$\overset{1}{\vee}$]... [$^{-}$] in (d) is followed by a new primary stress, and can be considered as terminal also. But let us see whether there are perhaps instances of rising pitches at level /^{1}/, falling pitches at levels /$^{2\ 3\ 4}$/, and possibly pitches that neither rise nor fall, all terminal. Consider the example *How do they study, now we've got their books?* This can be said thus, transcribing only stress, established pitch phonemes before each syllable, and the terminal phenomena now under consideration:

(f) *^{2}Hôw ^{2}dŏ ^{2}thèy ^{3}stú^{2}dy̆*[$^{\cdot\cdot}$] *^{2}nôw ^{2}wè've ^{2}gôt ^{2}thèir ^{3}bóo^{1}ks*[$^{-}$]*?*

This would seem to be the most frequent way of saying this in American English. If attention is to be centered on the problem they have in studying, it is likely that the sentence will be said this way:

(g) *^{2}Hôw ^{2}dŏ ^{2}thèy ^{3}stú^{1}dy̆*[$^{\cdot\cdot}$] *^{1}nôw ^{1}wè've ^{1}gôt ^{1}thèir ^{1}bóoks*[$^{-}$]*?*

Or the first part might be:

(h) *^{2}Hôw ^{2}dŏ ^{3}théy ^{1}stû^{1}dy*[$^{\cdot\cdot}$]...

If the question is asked with polite interest rather than insistence, it is likely to come out thus:

^{3}Hów ^{1}dŏ ^{1}thèy ^{1}stû^{1}dy̆[$^{\cdot\cdot}$] *^{1}nôw ^{1}wè've ^{1}gôt ^{1}thèir ^{1}bóoks*[$^{+}$]*?*

In the examples so far, we have noted a terminal instance of [$^{+}$] after [$\overset{1}{-}$], differing from [$^{-}$] after [$\overset{1}{\vee}$]. We have examples of sustention of pitches after [ˇ²] and [ˇ¹]. We then examine a British way of asking the above question:

(j) ³*Hôw* ²*dŏ* ²*thèy* ²*stú*²*dy̆*[⁺] ²*nôw* ²*wè've* ²*gôt* ²*thèir* ²*bóoks*[⁺]?

Here we have [⁺] twice after [²]. In British usage the other ways of saying this also exist, so that contrasting pitches are here found. Moreover, in American usage, example (i) could be said with /²/ instead of /¹/ everywhere, giving:

(k) ³*Hów* ²*dŏ* ²*thèy* ²*stû*²*dy̆*[¨] ²*nôw* ²*wè've* ²*gôt* ²*thèir* ²*bóoks*[⁺]?

Let us now look at two more examples; in answer to the question, *Where did you buy it?*, one could say either of the following:

(l) ²*Àt* ²*thĕ* ²*lîttlĕ* ³*már*²*kĕt*[¨] ²*nêar* ²*thĕ* ³*cór*¹*nĕr*[⁻].

(m) ²*Àt* ²*thĕ* ²*lîttlĕ* ³*már*²*kĕt*[⁺] ²*nêar* ²*thĕ* ³*cór*¹*ner*[⁻].

Example (l) ordinarily would have no punctuation after *market*, while a comma in the orthography of (m) would probably be reacted to with the rise after [²]. Here we have a direct contrast between [⁺] and [¨], in the same situations. In all the instances of terminal pitches, the absolute pitches as indicated are conditioned by the stress and can be left out of further account.

The phonemic analysis of the already found contrasts between [¨] and [⁺] after [²], and between [¨], [⁺], and [⁻] after [¹], will involve one of three possibilities: multiplication of the number of pitch phonemes (by three), analysis of at least the rises and falls as involving change to the adjacent pitch phoneme (necessitating setting up, at a minimum, an extra phoneme */⁵/), or considering the directions or contours of pitch as themselves phonemes distinct from the pitches. An examination of the details of the terminal contours gives the following facts: the exact pitch involved depends on the allophone of the pitch phoneme preceding the contour as a starting point; any rise reaches a point well below the next higher pitch (if there is one), and the absolute height reached is a function of the starting point; any sustention maintains pitch at the starting point until terminal silence is reached; any fall quickly moves down to silence. In other words, these contours seem to behave as allophones of entities whose phonetic characteristic is movement, rather than any particular pitch. Accordingly we analyze the phenomena marked [¨], [$^+$], [$^-$] as being three different manners of transition from the preceding part of the utterance to anything that may follow, and we set up three terminal junctures. [¨] is the principal phonetic characteristic of SINGLE-BAR juncture, /|/; [$^+$] is the characteristic of DOUBLE-BAR juncture, /||/; [$^-$] is the characteristic of DOUBLE-CROSS juncture /#/. These junctures are manners of terminating or going from parts of utterances. It remains to find instances of /^{3}/ before /|/, and of /^{2}/ and /^{3}/ before /#/.

If the question is asked whether one is reading a book by Macaulay, one says:

(n) ^{2}*Àre* ^{2}*yŏu* ^{2}*rêadĭng* ^{2}*Ma*^{3}*cáulay* ||.

But if the person addressed is named Macaulay and is asked whether he is reading, one says:

(o) ^{2}*Àre* ^{2}*yŏu* ^{3}*réadĭng*[¨] ^{3}*Măcáulăy* ||.

The [^{3}]...[¨] is terminal in the same way as similar instances of other pitches given above, and we analyze [^{3}]... [¨] as /^{3}..|/.

Now consider a mother calling her child:

(p) ^{3}*Jóhn* ^{2}*nўy*[$^-$].

(q) ^{2}*Jóhn* ^{3}*nўy*[$^-$].

Either of these may occur, with different effects. The terminal falls are instances of /#/ after /^{2}/ and /^{3}/ respectively.

In any of the illustrations having /^{3}/ before /|/, /||/, or /#/, we may substitute /^{4}/ and get exactly parallel results.

There are then the following pitch and contour phenomena at terminal points:

Pitch allophones	Contours [¨]	[$^{+}$]	[¯]	
$[\underset{\vee}{1}]$ $[\underset{\bullet}{1}]$ $[\underset{\wedge}{1}]$ $[\underline{1}]$	/^{1}|/	/^{1}||/	/^{1}#/	Phonemes
$[\underset{\vee}{2}]$ $[\underset{\bullet}{2}]$ $[\underset{\wedge}{2}]$ $[\underline{2}]$	/^{2}|/	/^{2}||/	/^{2}#/	Phonemes
$[\underset{\vee}{3}]$ $[\underset{\bullet}{3}]$ $[\underset{\wedge}{3}]$ $[\underline{3}]$	/^{3}|/	/^{3}||/	/^{3}#/	Phonemes
$[\underset{\vee}{4}]$ $[\underset{\bullet}{4}]$ $[\underset{\wedge}{4}]$ $[\underline{4}]$	/^{4}|/	/^{4}||/	/^{4}#/	Phonemes

The pitch allophones marked as to absolute pitch within any of the four levels have been seen to be conditioned by the stress. The change-points from one allophone to another, or from one pitch to another, have been marked as at the beginnings of syllables. In a linear notation this is inevitable. However, repeated observation leads to the conclusion that, as already noted, the change from syllable to syllable within the same level takes place in a smooth curve, so to speak, the actual movement being concentrated at the syllable boundaries between the end of one nucleus and the beginning of the next. When change is from one pitch level to a lower one, the movement can usually be described as smooth, though it may be quite rapid, particularly when the fall is from /^{3}/ to /^{1}/ on a one-syllable item. Examples are to be found in

(a) ^{2}*Hôw* ^{2}*dŏ* ^{2}*thèy* ^{3}*stú* ^{1}*dy̆#.*

On the other hand, the change from a lower to a higher pitch, as between *they* and *study* in this illustration, seems to actually take place at the beginning of the new syllable, and rather abruptly. Moreover, in an instance like

(b) ^{3}*Hôw* ^{2}*dŏ* ^{2}*thèy* ^{2}*stú*^{2}*dy̆*||.

the change from /^{3}/ to /^{2}/ after *how* also seems rather abrupt and clearly marked, in contrast with the usual smooth descent noticed above.

This leads to the conclusion that in the instance (a) ^{2}*Hôw* ^{2}*dŏ* ^{2}*thèy* ... there is, phonemically only ONE occurrence of the phoneme /^{2}/, and that this phoneme has scope. Its scope is statable as from the beginning of the utterance to the point where a higher pitch occurs. In the illustration (b) ending

... ^{2}*dŏ* ^{2}*thèy* ^{2}*stú*^{2}*dy̆*||

there is again ONE occurrence of /^{2}/, from the beginning of *do* until the final contour. In (a), ^{3}*stú*^{1}*dy̆* has an occurrence of /^{3}/ beginning at /stə́/, and an occurrence of /^{1}/ ending at /#/; the transition from /^{3}/ to /^{1}/ is not easily localizable, and falls rapidly but not abruptly. In this descent, there are actually points equal in absolute pitch to various allophones of /^{3}/ and /^{1}/ other than the initial and terminal ones, respectively, and to allophones of /^{2}/; but it must be noted that these points are not stable but in rapid movement, and we conclude that they are not in fact allophones of anything, but are characteristics of the pitches in normal transition. That is, there is NO occurrence of /^{2}/ between /^{3}/ and /^{1}/ in *study*. These phenomena, now precisely delimited, are best marked by writing a phonemic pitch symbol at the beginning of an utterance, writing a higher pitch phoneme when it occurs, and showing the following lower pitch phoneme at the end of its occurrence, thus:

(a) ^{2}*How do they* ^{3}*study*^{1}#

Now, in example (b), it will be necessary to write /^{2}/ at the point where it begins, since here the transition from /^{3}/ to /^{2}/ is of the more abrupt kind, and we interpret it as significant in regard to its point of beginning. In this example, no change from /^{2}/ occurs, and the completely unambiguous marking is as follows:

(b) ³*How* ²*do they study* ||

That is, the end pitch does not need to be marked.*

The statement of all the scope phenomena of pitch phonemes will be possible only after further research, but the general lines are as indicated here.

The juncture analysis made for /|/, /||/, and /#/ depends, be it noted, not on the pitch-level allophones, nor on the scope of the pitch, but on the presence of the positive segmentation points of sustention, rise, or fall. In the example (o) above, *Are you reading, Macaulay?*, the phonetic statement of pitch is: [²²³³··³³³+]. The places marked [¨] and [⁺] are the positive entities on which is based the juncture analysis. The pitch analysis is based on the levels and the change points; the first two symbols constitute one occurrence of /²/, the next two constitute one occurrence of /³/, then there is an occurrence of /|/, one occurrence of /³/ (three phonetic symbols), and one occurrence of /||/.

All the illustrative sentences given above are written out in full phonemic transcription in 1.8.

1.73. In the material examined above for the setting up of stress and juncture phenomena, it was observable that any sequence of vowels and consonants in normal transition or including plus junctures has only one primary stress, all other syllables having one of the other stresses. On the other hand, between any two successive primary stresses there is always one of the terminal junctures, and every primary stress is followed by one terminal juncture at some point subsequent to it.

Any utterance made in English ends in one of the terminal junctures. If it is a minimal complete utterance it has no other terminal junctures within it. In that case it must have one or more pitch phonemes, one--AND ONLY ONE --primary stress, and may have one or more other stresses and one or more plus junctures. If there are plus junctures, then there may be as many secondary stresses as there are pluses, but not more, and there may be less. Such a minimal complete utterance may be called by the

[* It was soon found necessary to mark end pitches, and in all our work since they are separately written.—GLT, HLS (1956).]

technical term PHONEMIC CLAUSE. Since all phonemic clauses must have one or more pitch phonemes and a terminal juncture, it is possible to take these off and leave an abstraction consisting only of segmental phonemes in normal transition or with pluses, accompanied by one primary and with the possibility of other stresses. Such an abstraction we call a PHONEMIC PHRASE. A phonemic phrase is unpronounceable, of course, but will turn out to be a very useful unit in our further analysis of the language. A phonemic phrase having no plus junctures (and consequently no secondary stresses) will be called a PHONEMIC WORD; it is the limiting case. These terms have, it must be noted, no connotation whatsoever of morphology; they are purely phonological. Examples of phonemic words are: *no* /nów/, *taker* /téykər/, *take 'er* /téykər/, *take it* /téykɨt/, *psychological* /sàykəlájikəl/. Phonemic phrases that are not phonemic words are: *White House* /wáyt+hæ̀ws/, *blackboard* /blǽk+bôhrd/, *old maid* /òwld+méyd/, *slyness* /sláy+nɨs/, *do you think so* /dɨ+yə+θíŋk+sôw/. Any of these can be turned into a phonemic clause, and thus made pronounceable, by adding pitches and a terminal juncture.

1.8. The phonemes of English have been shown to be the following:

vowels: /i e æ ɨ ə a u o ɔ/;

consonants: /p t k b d g c j f θ s š v ð z ž m n ŋ l r w y h/;

stresses: /´ ˆ ` ˘/;

internal juncture: /+/;

pitches: /¹ ² ³ ⁴/;

terminal junctures: /| || #/;

A full phonemic transcription of all the examples used in 1.71, 1.72, and 1.73 serves to illustrate the use of the phonemes:

(a) /²hæ̂w+də+ðèy+³stə́diy¹#/

(b) /³hæ̂w+²də+ðèy+stə́diy||/

(c) /³hǽw+də+ðèy+stə̂diy¹#/

(d) /^{3}hǽw+də+ðèy+stə̂diy^{1}#^{1}ðén#/

(e) /^{3}hǽw+də+ðèy+stə̂diy||/

(aa) /^{2}hæ̂w+də+ðèy+^{4}stə́diy^{1}#/

(bb) /^{4}hæ̂w+^{2}də+ðèy+stə́diy||/

(cc) /^{4}hǽw+də+ðèy+stə̂diy^{1}#/

(dd) /^{4}hæ̌w+də+ðèy+stə̂diy^{1}#^{1}ðén#/

(ee) /^{4}hǽw+də+ðèy+stə̂diy||/

(f) /^{2}hæ̂w+də+ðèy+^{3}stə́diy^{2}| ^{2}næ̂w+wìyv+gât+ðèhr+^{3}búks^{1}#/

(g) /^{2}hæ̂w+də+ðèy+^{3}stə́diy^{1}| ^{1}næ̂w+wìyv+gât+ðèhr+búks#/

(h) /^{2}hæ̂w+də+^{3}ðéy+stə̂diy^{1}| ^{1}næ̂w+wìyv+gât+ðèhr+búks#/

(i) /^{3}hǽw+də+ðèy+stə̂diy^{1}| ^{1}næ̂w+wìyv+gât+ðèhr+búks||/

(j) /^{3}hæ̂w+də+ðèy+stə́diy^{2}||^{2}næ̂w+wìyv+gât+ðèhr+búks||/

(k) /^{3}hǽw+də+ðèy+stə̂diy^{2}| ^{2}næ̂w+wìyv+gât+ðèhr+búks||/

(l) /^{2}æ̀t+ðə+lîtəl+^{3}márkɨt^{2}| ^{2}nîhr+ðə+^{3}kóhnər^{1}#/

(m) /^{2}æ̀t+ðə+lîtəl+^{3}márkɨt^{2}||^{2}nîhr+ðə+^{3}kóhnər^{1}#/

(n) /^{2}àhr+yə+rîydiŋ+mə^{3}kóhliy||/

(o) /^{2}àhr+yə+^{3}ríydiŋ| ^{3}məkóhliy||/

(p) /^{3}jániy^{2}#/

(q) /^{2}já^{3}niy#/

In previous treatments of or allusions to English stress and intonation, there is often mention of such items as 'declarative sentence intonation', 'interrogative intonation', 'contrastive stress', and others. Our treatment of pitch should serve to show conclusively that on the phonemic level one has to deal with pitch phonemes occurring at stated places in utterances and with stated scopes. All the above examples from (a) to (k) are questions, but they exhibit several different types of pitch sequences; and the sequences they have occur also in sentences that are not questions. True, all the sequences and combinations that do occur could be listed, and it would be found that they can be tied up in various ways with the type of sentence and its meaning; but such tie-ups are in the field of syntax, or even beyond, in metalinguistics. On the level of phonemics there are no such things as 'intonations'.

As for 'contrastive stress', the facts are that when emphasis is desired on any part of an utterance, several procedures can be used. First, the primary stress can be put on any part of a phonemic phrase: compare examples (g) and (h)--*How do they stúdy* ... and *How do théy study* ...; one could also say *Hów do they study* ... (examples c,d,e), or *How dó they study* ... Secondly, when one wishes to emphasize the item that already has primary stress, one can raise the pitch from /^{3}/ to /^{4}/: examples (a) and (aa). Third, the low pitch as on *then* in (d) is a kind of emphasis. Fourth, one can contrast two items by having /^{3}/ on the principal one, /^{2}/ on the other, or, with greater emphasis /^{4}/ and /^{3}/: *I said* ^{3}*Joe, not* ^{2}*Bill* or *I said* ^{4}*Joe, not* ^{3}*Bill;* the contrast is in pitch, of course, not stress (and there are other ways of saying these sentences). Fifth, one can say the whole utterance, or certain parts of it, with greatly increased loudness and accompanying extra high,or, in some cases, extra low, pitch; this is often represented by special typography: *I said* JOE, *not Bill*. When this happens, the whole utterance or portion of it is stretched out horizontally and vertically, as it were; this is then the point at which we draw the line between microlinguistics and metalinguistics: the phenomena that are segmentable were analyzed as phonemes of one kind or another; the phenomena that transcend segments are now stated to be metalinguistic, matters of style, and not part of the microlinguistic analysis. Here, then, phonology ends.

A final recapitulation may now be made: vowel, consonant, and stress phonemes have allophones statable in terms of position in the sequence; plus juncture and pitch phonemes have allophones statable in terms of stress sequences; terminal junctures have allophones statable in terms of the pitch preceding them. Other phenomena are metalinguistic and describable only in terms of the whole microlinguistic analysis.

PART II. MORPHEMICS.

2. When the phonological analysis of a language has been made, the next point to consider is what use one can make of it for further analysis. It is taken for granted that further analysis is necessary and possible: knowing the phonological system of a language does not tell us anything about the way the phonological units are used. Saying this does not, however, lead to the conclusion that we are then immediately to become concerned with the 'meaning' of the linguistic material. It simply means that we have to look for further structural systems on levels other than the phonological.

Inspection of the linguistic material shows immediately that similar sequences or combinations of phonemes keep recurring. The recurrences exhibit patterns of occurrence and distribution. And from time to time recurrent gaps in distribution are noted. We say then that the analysis we are now going to do, the MORPHEMICS of the language, deals with the recurring patterned partials in utterances. These partials are made up of one or more phonemes. The distributional gaps are often found to pattern as if they were themselves partials with phonemic content, and are then set up as zero-elements.

The recurring partials, including zero-elements, are the MORPHEMES of a language. They are determined by processes parallel to those used in phonology: inspection, commutation within a frame, complementary distribution. There is, however, no criterion parallel to that of phonetic similarity, for phonemic similarity is not a necessary basis for classifying morphemes: different morphemes may be homonymous, or the variants of one morpheme may have very different phonemic shapes, or some variants may be zero phonemically; illustrations will be given below.

The morphemic analysis should be based on the fullest possible phonological statement in order to be complete. It is true that incomplete morphemic analyses can be made from phonologically inadequate data, or even in the absence of such data; but all such analyses are defective in direct proportion to the amount of phonological analysis omitted. In these terms, all existing morphemic analyses are defective, being based on traditional writing systems, or on phonemic statements that disregard or omit systematic and complete treatment of all or part of the accentual, junctural, and intonational phenomena. This is not to say that in the actual procedure of analyzing a language there is not a constant going back and forth between phonology and morphemics, with refinements and corrections being made in either direction. But the analyst must at all times be aware of the level-differences, and the systematic presentation must always be made in terms of the logical sequence, in one linear order, with the levels carefully distinguished.

In the present state of morphemic analysis it is often convenient to use the meanings of utterance fractions as a general guide and short-cut to the identification of morphemes. This is especially so in the case of languages that are more or less well known to the analyst, as has been true for most morphemic work done up to now. When we are confronted, however, with a language that we know little about in terms of the relation of the linguistic behavior of the speakers to the rest of their cultural behavior, it becomes clear that meaning can be of little help as a guide. The theoretical basis of the analysis then becomes evident: it consists of the recognition of the recurrences and distributions of similar patterns and sequences. The analyst must therefore constantly keep in mind this theoretical basis, and must be aware that his hunches about what goes with what are really short-cut conclusions about distributional facts.

Morphemes may have variants in different situations. These are the ALLOMORPHS. The statement of all the forms of the morphemes of a language is the MORPHOPHONEMICS. The statement of the sequences of morphemes that occur is the ARRANGEMENT (also called TACTICS). In English, as in many other languages, it is found to be convenient to dichotomize morphemes into bases and all others (see below), and then to treat morpheme-sequences that involve only one base under one heading--MORPHOLOGY, and those that involve more than one base under another--SYNTAX. The term GRAMMAR can be used to include the whole of the analysis of a language --phonology and morphemics. One of the concomitants of the morphophonemics is a list of all the morphemes of a language--THE LEXICON.

A full presentation would begin with the recording of the behavior events--the actually occurring allomorphs, in their several phonemic forms. These would then be classified and arranged by the morphophonemic relationships into the lexicon. Then would follow the statement of the arrangements. No such full grammar is attempted here. The purpose is to present enough material for discussion to illustrate the procedures and techniques involved.

2.1. Examination of the language shows that English morphemes may be classified as follows on the basis of their phonological make-up and their role in morphology or syntax.

SEGMENTAL morphemes: consist of vowels and/or consonants (including semivowels) in normal transition; zero allomorphs are included here. Segmental morphemes are the basis of the morphological structure.

SUPRASEGMENTAL morphemes: consist of sequences of stress phonemes with or without plus junctures; or of sequences of pitch phonemes with a terminal juncture. There are no zero allomorphs here. Some suprasegmental morphemes enter into morphological structures; most of them, however, are in the realm of syntax.

2.11. Segmental morphemes are divided into two types: BASES and SUFFIXES. Bases come first in a morpheme-complex. The number of bases is large, and the list cannot be exhaustively stated. English bases are the part of the structure usually described as having the 'meaning' of the item. Bases are classifiable further by whether they do or do not combine with suffixes; and if they do, by the suffix-sets that enter into the combinations. Certain bases in English of limited distribution occur principally as the first item of a multibase sequence: they are usually called prefixes, but as their functioning is different from that of affixes as a whole, the term PRE-BASE is here preferred. Examples of bases follow (√ is read 'morpheme'; base morphemes are shown with a terminal hyphen): √mehn-, √huw-, √gud-, √duw-, √in-, √ænd-, √næw-, √ow-; pre-bases are: √bɨ-, √ə-, √diy-, √mis-, √kan-, etc. (these can be exhaustively listed).

Suffixes are of at least two kinds: FINAL (or inflectional), and NON-FINAL (or derivational). They follow bases. Non-final suffixes form STEMS from bases; stems behave with final suffixes as do bases, so that a stem is an extended base, consisting of a base followed by one or more non-final suffixes. Final suffixes are added to bases and stems in sets; these sets, or inflections, are the basis for classifying bases and stems into the so-called 'parts of speech'. The sets of inflected or derived forms of a base are PARADIGMS. All suffixes can be exhaustively listed; examples of non-final suffixes are: √-nɨs-, √-ər-, √-ɨtiy-, √-hud-, √-dəm-, √-eyšən-; of final suffixes: √-z, √-s, √-ɨz, √-d, √-iŋ, etc.

2.12. Suprasegmental morphemes consisting of patterns of stress, with the possibility of including plus junctures, are called SUPERFIXES. Those consisting of pitches and a terminal juncture are called INTONATION PATTERNS.

English superfixes always contain one--and only one--primary stress. In addition they may contain one or more plus junctures, and one or more stresses other than primary.

A morpheme-complex consisting of a single base, its accompanying suffixes (if any), and a superfix, is called a (MORPHEMIC) WORD. This is the primary unit of morphology as contrasted with morphemics as a whole, whose unit is the morpheme, or with syntax, where the unit is the MORPHEMIC PHRASE.

A morphemic phrase consists of two or more bases, with their suffixes, and a superfix. But it must be noted that the bases in a phrase have to be considered as words first, in order to make the analysis of the phrase. That is, one cannot simply consider the phrase as a sequence of bases (with or without suffixes), and a superfix, because the phrase superfix is found to be statable always in terms of the morphological nature of the included words and as an element superseding their superfixes in accordance with regular correlations. On the addition of an intonation pattern to a phrase we get a MORPHEMIC CLAUSE; this is wholly in the realm of syntax. Intonation patterns always contain at least one pitch phoneme, and end in one of the terminal junctures.

There is a hierarchy of relationship and analytical primacy in these various kinds of morphemes: intonation patterns depend for their scope and exact form on the phrase-superfixes; the phrase-superfixes depend on the word-superfixes; the word-superfixes depend on the base-and-suffix combinations.

Examples of superfixes as such are: √-´ in *go*, √-´˘ in *under*, √´+` in *blackbird*, √^+`+´ in *Do it now*, etc. Examples of intonation patterns, for the segmental and superfixal filling-in of which see 1.8, are: √^{231}#, √^{32}||, √^{3}||, √^{241}#, etc.

Examples of words can now be given. The symbol & is read 'combined with', → means 'results in', ^{w}√ means 'morphemic word'. *Man* has the formula: √mehn- & √-´ → ^{w}√méhn; *taker* is: √teyk- & √-ər- & √-´˘ → ^{w}√téykər; *slynesses* is: √slay- & √-nɨs- & √-ɨz & √-´+˘˘ → ^{w}√slay+nɨsɨz (or the superfix may be √-´˘˘ giving ^{w}√sláynɨsɨz).

Examples of phrases are (^{ps}√ means 'phrase-superfix'; these are also written without hyphens under the primary stress, in contrast with word superfixes which have a hyphen; ^{p}√ means 'phrase'): *take her* is ^{w}√téyk & ^{w}√hə́hr & ^{ps}√´+` → ^{p}√téyk+hə̀hr; or the superfix may be ^{ps}√^+´, giving ^{p}√têyk+hə́hr; or it may be ^{ps}√´˘, giving ^{p}√téykər. These with intonation patterns (^{i}√) become clauses (^{c}√): ^{p}√téyk+hə̀hr & ^{i}√^{31}# → ^{c}√^{3}téyk+hə̀hr^{1}#; ^{p}√têyk+hə́hr & ^{i}√^{231}# → ^{c}√^{2}têyk+^{3}hə́hr^{1}#; ^{p}√téykər & ^{i}√^{31}# → ^{c}√^{3}téykər^{1}#. Other intonation patterns may occur, of course, with this phrase.

2.13. The terms *word, phrase, clause* have been used in this Outline with the modifier *phonemic* in 1.73, and with *morphemic* just now in 2.12. It is in point to see how the items so differentiated differ and function.

Phonemic words have no plus junctures: *taker, take 'er, Plato* said as /pléytòw/ or /pléytow/. Phonemic phrases include plus junctures: *take her* as /téyk+hə̀hr/ or /têyk+hə̌hr/, *Plato* as /pléy+tòw/. Phonemic clauses include pitches and a terminal juncture: /^{3}téykər^1#/, /^{2}têyk+^{3}hə́hr^1#/. Every phonemic clause is coterminous with a phonemic phrase or word. A phonemic word is a limiting case of a phonemic phrase. All three units are in the realm of phonemics.

Morphemic words have one base: *taker, Plato.* This is the realm of morphology. Morphemic phrases have more than one base, each as a word: *take her, take 'er.* Morphemic clauses have an intonation pattern added to a morphemic phrase. Morphemic phrases and clauses are in the realm of syntax. These three units are all under morphemics, in a hierarchy of inclusiveness.

A summarizing table may now be given, omitting consideration of clauses (← 'resulting from'):

A phonemic word may be:
- a morphemic word: /téykər/ = $^{w}\surd$téykər ← √teyk- & √-ər- & √-́˘;
- a morphemic phrase: /téykər/ = $^{p}\surd$téykər ← $^{w}\surd$téyk & $^{w}\surd$hə́hr & $^{ps}\surd$́˘.

A morphemic word may be:
- a phonemic word: √hay- & √-nɨs- & √-́˘ → $^{w}\surd$háynɨs = /háynɨs/;
- a phonemic phrase: √slay-& √-nɨs- & √-́+˘ → $^{w}\surd$sláy+nɨs = /sláy+nɨs/.

A phonemic phrase may be:
- a morphemic word: *slyness;*
- a morphemic phrase: *take her.*

A morphemic phrase may be:
- a phonemic word: *take 'er;*
- a phonemic phrase: *take her.*

2.14. Within morphemic phrases, as has been seen above, words may appear in alternants of special phonemic shape. As far as the stresses involved are concerned, this is taken care of by the setting up of phrase-superfixes as one of the constituent elements of a phrase; the relation of the phrase-superfixes to the word-superfixes is, as has been said, a matter of syntax. With certain phrase-superfixes some words appear in phonemic shapes involving loss or replacement of the segmental phonemes (the so-called weak forms of auxiliaries, personal pronouns, prepositions, and others--e.g., /s/ for /íz/ in *it's*, /ɨm/ for /hím/ in *see 'im*, /tə/ for /túw/ in *to me*); these must be analyzed as words within phrases--as syntax. The special contractions or portmanteau forms that arise at times (/donów/ for /dównt/ from /dùw+nát/ and /nów/) are instances of the same processes.. All such special phrase alternants involve more than simple allomorphic alternation, and are to be considered as results of alternation of the already fully constituted morphemic word. We call such alternants of words ALLOLOGS, and consider them more fully in 4ff.

Once we have stated the above definitions of words and phrases and clauses on the morphemic level, and have established allologs, thus taking into consideration both phonemic and morphemic structure, but independently, we have substantiated the sharp delimitation of the fields of morphology (word-structure) and syntax (phrase-structure) in English.

2.2. The morphophonemics of English involves extensive statements of the alternations of form of morphemes under varying conditions.

Bases are taken as not themselves inherently consisting of a group of allomorphs, but as exhibiting morphophonemic alternation only under the influence (= in the presence) of certain kinds of, or specific suffixes and superfixes. That is, there is a reciprocal relation, in that certain base allomorphs are called for in the presence of certain suffixes, or that certain suffix allomorphs appear automatically in the presence of bases of a stated phonological structure (that is, generally, but not for specific bases).

Suffixes, especially inflectional ones, usually have many allomorphs. Superfixes have few allomorphs, generally involving the alternation of normal transition and plus juncture, with some stress alternations (especially /ˆ/ and /`/). Intonation patterns show allomorphs involving the scope of each of the pitch phonemes--that is, the extent of the material included under each pitch.

The actual discussion of English morphophonemics will not be taken up here except in terms of some specific morphemes that will be treated below. A full study would involve statements about the kinds of consonant and vowel sequences that occur, the relation of certain stresses to specific segmental phoneme structure, and the relation of intonations to the stresses and junctures; then would follow a morpheme list with all allomorphs, and an indefinitely extendable list of morphemes not showing alternation.

3.1. Base morphemes are found which are associated with different suffix-sets as in these examples:

> *child, child's, children, children's;*
> *they, them, their, theirs;*
> *great, greater, greatest;*
> *do, does, did, done, doing.*

These four types may be called by their traditional names: NOUNS, (PERSONAL) PRONOUNS, ADJECTIVES, VERBS. Nouns show inflection for SINGULAR and PLURAL NUMBERS, and for POSSESSIVE CASE (the form is determined by the number, so that this order of statement is necessary--see below). Pronouns show OBJECT case and two kinds of possessive. Adjectives show COMPARATIVE and SUPERLATIVE. Verbs are inflected for 3D PERSON SG. NON-PAST, PAST, PAST PARTICIPLE, PRESENT PARTICIPLE. There is also the verb *be*, showing a special form for 1st sg. non-past, different sg. and pl. past forms, a special plural non-past form. The uninflected or name-form is the base.

In the discussion below, these additional morphemic symbols are used: $\sqrt[a]{}$ 'allomorph'; ~ 'alternates with'.

3.2. Noun inflectional suffixes are:

Plural: $\sqrt{}$-Z^{1}: $^{a}\sqrt{}$-s after bases ending in /p t k f θ/;

$^{a}\sqrt{}$-ɨz (or -əz, -iz) after bases ending in /s z š ž c j/;

$^{a}\sqrt{}$-z elsewhere (except in the 'irregular' instances that have to be listed).

These three are the regular automatic alternants. The following are the principal irregular allomorphs, which should be accompanied by lists (which can usually be made exhaustive):

$^{a}\sqrt{}$-s$_{2}$, as in *dice;*

$^{a}\sqrt{}$-ɨz$_{2}$, with voicing of stem-final /s/: *houses;*

$^{a}\sqrt{}$-z$_{2}$, with voicing of stem-final /f θ/; *knives, paths;*

$^{a}\sqrt{}$-ən, as in *oxen, brethren;*

$^{a}\sqrt{}$-rən, as in *children;*

$^{a}\sqrt{}$-Ø [read Ø as 'zero'], as in *sheep, deer, fish;*

$^{a}\sqrt{}$(Ṽ)-Ø, that is, zero with alternation of the stem-vowel, as in *feet, mice;*

$^{a}\sqrt{}^{L}$ ('loss of final consonant'), as in *data, phenomena;*

$^{a}\sqrt{}$(is > iyz): *crises;*

$^{a}\sqrt{}$(əs > ay), often with consonant change: *fungi;*

$^{a}\sqrt{}$(ə > iy): *alumnae;*

etc., etc.

Possessive: $\sqrt{}$-Z^{2}: $^{a}\sqrt{}$-s, $^{a}\sqrt{}$-ɨz, $^{a}\sqrt{}$-z distributed as for $\sqrt{}$-Z^{1} for singular nouns and for plurals not ending in the allomorphs $^{a}\sqrt{}$-s, $^{a}\sqrt{}$-ɨz, $^{a}\sqrt{}$-z of $\sqrt{}$Z^{1}; but in singular proper names ending in /z/ the alternant is, with many speakers, $^{a}\sqrt{}$-Ø: *tack's, horse's, bag's, men's, James's* or *James';*

$^{a}\sqrt{}$-Ø with plurals ending in the allomorphs $^{a}\sqrt{}$-s, $^{a}\sqrt{}$-ɨz, $^{a}\sqrt{}$-z of $^{a}\sqrt{}$Z^{1}: *boys'.*

3.3. The English personal pronouns have the following forms in our dialects:

	Subject	*Object*	*1st possessive*	*2d possessive*
Sg 1	áy	míy	máy	máyn
Pl 1	wíy	ə́s	áhr	áhrz
Sg 3M	híy	hím	híz	híz
F	šíy	hə́hr	hə́hr	hə́hrz
Nt	ít	ít	íts	íts
2	yúw	yúw	yúhr (HLS: yóhr)	yúhrz (HLS: yóhrz)
Pl 3	ðéy	ðém	ðéhr	ðéhrz
Interrog.	húw	húw(m)	húwz	húwz

The Pl 1 possessives are /ǽw(ə)r(z)/, (/áw(ə)r(z)/) with some speakers; the 2 possessives are /yóhr(z)/ with many speakers. In substandard speech 2d possessives /áhrn hízən hə́hrn yúhrn~ yóhrn ðéhrn/ are encountered. The object form of /húw/ most often occurs without /m/ in colloquial usage.

These forms represent a small closed relic pattern, and further analysis of them is useful as an illustration of method. Such analysis gives these results:

The bases are: ª√a-~ª√mVy-; ª√wi-~ª√ə-~ª√a- (or ª√aw- or ª√æw-); √hi-; ª√ši-~√hə-; √it-; √yuw-; √ðe-; √huw-.

The suffixes are: subject, ª√-y~ª√-Ø; object, ª√-m~ª√-Ø~ª√-s~ª√-r~ª√(V=i)-Ø; 1st possessive, ª√-z~ª√-s~ª√-r~√(V=a)-Ø; 2d possessive, ª√-z~ª√-Ø~ª√-n. A subject suffix is set up on the basis of the presence of /-y/ in five of the eight forms, and in two of them--/híy ðéy/--clearly as an addition to the base. The object suffix ª√-m is clear, and the pattern requires the other allomorphs. ª√-r is set up because object /hə́hr/ is identical with possessive /hə́hr/; ª√-s could be eliminated by setting up the base alternant ª√əs- for Pl 1, and extending the suffix allomorph ª√-Ø to cover both the vowel manifestation in Sg 1 and the base change in Pl 1. The 1st possessive is regular √-Z^2 in /híz íts/, and the other forms may be considered further special allomorphs of √-Z^2. The allomorph ª√-r automatically calls for a preceding /h/ after the base vowel in the dialect here represented; the /h/ is added to a simple base vowel, and replaces /w/ of a /VS/ sequence. The 2d possessive may be considered a separate morpheme; the allomorph ª√-∅ (in /híz íts húwz/ may be eliminated by considering that these forms have ª√-z, which, however, in normal transition after /z s/ is automatically reduced to absence of a phoneme.

Here also may be illustrated a technique of identifying morphemes by numerical symbols in a systematic way. Let us number the bases 10, 20, 30, 40, 50, 60, 70, 80, for Sg 1, Pl 1, Sg 3 M, F, Nt, 2, Pl 3, Interrogative respectively. Where there are alternants they are numbered 11, 12; 21, 22, 23; 41, 42. The suffixes are numbered .010 subject, .020 object, .110 1st possessive, .120 2d possessive; allomorphs are .011, .012; .021, .022, .023, .024, .025; .111, .113, .114, .115; .121, .122, .123. The resulting combinations are:

Sg 1:	11.011,	12.025,	12.115,	12.115.123.	
Pl 1:	21.011,	22.023,	23.114,	23.114.121.	
Sg 3 M:	30.011,	30.021,	30.111,	30.111.122.	
F:	41.011,	42.024,	42.114,	42.114.121.	
N:	50.012,	50.022,	50.113,	50.113.122.	
2:	60.012,	60.022,	60.114,	60.114.121.	
Pl 3:	70.011,	70.021,	70.114,	70.114.121.	
Interr.:	80.012,	80.021, (.012),	80.111,	80.111.122.	

Statements about automatic /h/ have to be made for forms involving .024 and .114.

All these pronoun forms have the superfix √´

The archaic pronoun *thou* is analyzed into a base ª√ðaw- (or ª√ðæw-) ~ª√ðVy-, with the suffixes ª√-∅, ª√(V=i)-∅, ª√(V=a) -∅, ª√-n: 91.012, 92.025. 92.115, 92.115.123.

The weak forms /˘ɨm ˘əm ˘ər/ etc. are not allomorphs but allologs, and are treated under the syntax, below.

3.4. The adjective inflections are:

√-ər comparative;
√-ɨst (or √-əst or √-ist) superlative.

These occur with almost complete regularity, and involve very few base alternations and have few allomorphs:

good, *better*--$^{a}\sqrt{}$bet- & $^{a}\sqrt{}$-ər, *best*--$^{a}\sqrt{}$be(t)- & $^{a}\sqrt{}$-st;
bad, *worse*--$^{a}\sqrt{}$wər- & $^{a}\sqrt{}$-s, *worst*--$^{a}\sqrt{}$wər- & $^{a}\sqrt{}$-st;
much, *more*--$^{a}\sqrt{}$mow- & $^{a}\sqrt{}$-r (→$^{w}\sqrt{}$móhr), *most*--$^{a}\sqrt{}$mow- & $^{a}\sqrt{}$-st;
etc., etc.

By adjective is here meant, of course, any item that has this inflection, and those that do not (e.g. *beautiful*) are excluded on the morphological level.

3.5. Verb inflectional suffixes are:

Sg 3d non-past: $\sqrt{}$-Z^{3}: $^{a}\sqrt{}$-s, $^{a}\sqrt{}$-ɨz, $^{a}\sqrt{}$-z as for $\sqrt{}$-Z^{1} and $\sqrt{}$-Z^{2};
: $^{a}\sqrt{}$-z_{2} with base-change in $\sqrt{}$sey-, $\sqrt{}$duw-, $\sqrt{}$hæv-, giving /séz dəz hǽz/;
: $^{a}\sqrt{}$-Ø in *will*, *shall*, *can*, *may*, *must*, *ought*, and *need* and *dare* in some circumstances.

past: $\sqrt{}$-D^{1}: $^{a}\sqrt{}$-t after bases ending in /p k c f θ s š/;
: $^{a}\sqrt{}$-ɨd after bases ending in /d t/;
: $^{a}\sqrt{}$-d elsewhere except irregularly as below;
: $^{a}\sqrt{}$-t_{2} with base change, as in *thought*, *bought*, *slept*, *built*, *went*;
: $^{a}\sqrt{}$-t_{3} without base change, as in *spelt*, *burnt*;
: $^{a}\sqrt{}$-d_{2} with base change, as in *sold*, *said*, *did*;
: $^{a}\sqrt{}$-Ø, subdivided by kinds of base change, as in *come--came*, *take--took*, *cut--cut*, *sing--sang* (a complete listing includes some 260 verbs in a few dozen small classes).

past participle: $\sqrt{}$-D^{2}: $^{a}\sqrt{}$-t, $^{a}\sqrt{}$-ɨd, $^{a}\sqrt{}$-d as for $\sqrt{}$-D^{1};
: $^{a}\sqrt{}$-t_{2}, $^{a}\sqrt{}$-t_{3}, $^{a}\sqrt{}$-d_{2} as for $\sqrt{}$-D^{1};
: $^{a}\sqrt{}$-(ə)n, as in *taken*, *shown*, etc.

: $\sqrt[a]{}$-Ø as in *come, cut, sung* (subdivided as for √-D[1]; the combination of the two lists results in a smaller total number of subclasses).

present participle: √-iŋ—always regular, no allomorphs, and no base changes (but a few verbs--*will, shall*, etc., do not have this form and also lack the form with √-D[2]; /ɨn/ is a syntactic result).

The verb *be* has the inflections: Sg 1 n.-p. /ǽm/ (or /éhm/ or /ǽhm/), Sg 3 n.-p. /íz/, Pl n.-p. /áhr/, Sg past /wə́z/, Pl p. /wə́hr/, p.pt. /bín/ (or bíyn/), pr.pt. /bíyiŋ/. These forms can be analyzed thus:

$\sqrt[a]{}$æ- (or $\sqrt[a]{}$eh-) 'non-past (other than Sg 3) of *be*' & √-m 'Sg 1 subject';

$\sqrt[a]{}$i- 'Sg 3 non-past of *be*' & √-Z[3];

$\sqrt[a]{}$æ- becoming automatically /ah/ before √-r 'Pl subject';

$\sqrt[a]{}$wə- 'past of *be*' & √-Z[3] (here extended to cover all Sg subjects);

$\sqrt[a]{}$wə- & √-r 'Pl subject' (with automatic /h/ before /r/;

$\sqrt[a]{}$bi- & $\sqrt[a]{}$-n (allomorph of √-D[2]);

√biy- & √-iŋ.

All these forms except the last have the superfix √-´; the last has √-´˘. This is again a small relic inflection, interesting chiefly for its methodological implications.

The verb *be*, with a few others, has special allologs in many constructions.

3.6. English word-superfixes are morphemes that do not seem to be directly connected with the nature or behavior of the bases or stems that they go with. A few pairs like *cónvict* and *convíct*, noun and verb respectively, do not establish any overwhelming pattern. In derivation, there are such relations as are seen in *várĭŏus: văríĕtў*; when extensive studies of the morphophonemics of English derivation have been made, it will be possible to be more specific in this matter.

Examination of a considerable body of evidence, however, does indicate that in most instances where weak stresses occur at the beginning of a superfix before a strong stress, the weak syllables involve allologs of prepositions, articles, the verbs *be* or *have* (or other auxiliaries), pre-bases, and so on; in such cases there are rarely more than two such weak syllables. In the instances where there are no allologs of the types mentioned involved, there is never more than one weak syllable, and the base is found to be one in which the initial syllable appears in other morphophonemic forms under strong stress with other superfixes. Where the base has more than one syllable before the one that has primary stress, there will always be a tertiary stress on the second syllable before the primary. In most instances of superfixes beginning √ˋ˘ ..., however, there will be more than one base under the superfix.

This situation is indicative of the fact that word-superfixes and phrase-superfixes are often of identical shapes. The shortest superfixes are more likely to be word-superfixes. The longest are exclusively phrase-superfixes. Those involving secondary stress, whether long or short, are generally phrase-superfixes. Outside of these limitations it is not possible, without much further study, to classify the English superfixes as word-forming, phrase-forming, or both. Accordingly, only a sampling of superfixes will be given, with indication of the kinds of words or phrases they go with.

Superfixes with initial primary followed only by weaks are:

√–́ in *go* (word), √́ in *don't* (phrase);
√–́˘ : *under*, √́˘ : *doesn't*;
√–́˘˘ : *animal*, √́˘˘ : *isn't it* /ízəntɨt/;
√–́˘˘˘ : *culturally*, √́˘˘˘ : *sharpening it* /šárpəniŋɨt/.

Primary-initial superfixes with other following stresses are:

√´ˋ : *contents;*

√´˘ˋ : *animate* /ǽnɨmèyt/;

√´˘ˋ˘: *operator.*

Superfixes beginning with other than primary are:

√˘´ : *across*

√˘´˘ : *Virginia,* √˘´˘ : *containing;*

√ˋ´ : *verbose;*

√ˋ˘´˘: *operation;* √ˋ˘´˘ : *condescension.*

The superfixes involving /+/ and those with /ˆ/ (which always have /+/) follow the same kinds of patterns.

3.7. Derivational (non-final or stem-forming) suffixes may be best classified in terms of the inflectional class of the stems formed with them. That is, there will be noun-forming, adjective-forming, and verb-forming suffixes, as well as some others. The results are, on the addition of the appropriate superfixes and inflectional suffixes, words, and then enter into phrases as do words of simpler structure.

A full treatment of English derivation would be extremely long and complex, often involving statements of morphophonemic alternation in both suffix and base, and tying it in frequently with different possible superfixes. Not even initial descriptions exist. The present study is not a complete grammar of English, and we therefore omit any further consideration of derivation.

4. The scope of syntax has been indicated above in 2 and 2.14. In the present tentative discussion, an attempt is made to set forth some of the procedures by which we believe syntax will come to bo done, and to illustrate certain selected portions of English syntax. The treatment will necessarily be uneven and inadequate. But it will show the ineffectiveness of much of what has been called syntactic analysis hitherto, and may indicate the problems yet to be resolved.

The procedures for syntactic analysis do not differ essentially from those already used. With the phonology completely established, and the morphological analysis completed, the syntax of a language like English can be constructed objectively, without the intervention of translation meaning or any resort to metalinguistic phenomena.

Utterances are analyzed syntactically about as follows: A phonemic transcription is made first; this determines the portions of utterance that can be separated out and treated as units, namely the phonemic clauses. The units thus determined are the first IMMEDIATE CONSTITUENTS. Then, within each phonemic clause the intonation patterns are separated from the phonemic phrases and within each phonemic phrase the constituents delimited by plus-junctures are noted, and a hierarchy in terms of the stresses (primary, secondary, tertiary [all strong]; weak) is established. This leads to the separation of the superfix for each phrase, leaving a set of phrase fractions, including portmanteau items. Attention now turns to the phrase fractions, which are examined in the light of the already available morphemic analysis, and their constituents are determined. When all the allologs and words are established, we then resort to the usual substitution techniques. After that, statements can be made describing the constructions that occur, in terms of classes of words, allologic changes in the presence of phrase superfixes, classes of superfixes, intonation patterns, and order and concord. It is emphasized that all this is done without the use of 'meaning': it is formal analysis of formal units. In fact, it becomes evident that any real approach to meaning must be based upon the existence of such an objective syntax, rather than the other way round (cf. 5.1).

4.1. In order to establish the terminology and symbology to be used in syntactic analysis we shall consider a number of examples in detail.

Let us take the sentence:

Long Island is a long island.

The phonemic transcription is:

/^{2}lòhŋ+^{3}áylənd^{2}| ^{2}iz(+)ə+lôhŋ+^{3}áylənd^{1}#/

There are two phonemic clauses here:

/^{2}lòhŋ+^{3}áylənd^{2}|/; and

/^{2}iz(+)ə+lôhŋ+^{3}áylənd #/.

By definition, they are stated to be coterminous with SYNTACTIC CLAUSES. These syntactic clauses consist of an intonation pattern and a SYNTACTIC PHRASE.

In order to facilitate use of the symbology about to be presented, it is best at this point to make some recapitulating statements. The phonemic word consists of segmental and stress phonemes:

$/W/ = /Ph_{seg}, Ph_{str}/.$

The phonemic phrase consists of segmental and stress phonemes, and plus junctures:

$/P/ = /Ph_{seg}, Ph_{str}, + /.$

The phonemic clause consists of a phonemic phrase (including phonemic words) along with pitch phonemes and a terminal juncture:

$/Cl/ = /P, Ph_{pi}, Ph_{tj}/.$

In these three entities there are seen two levels of organization within phonemics: the word and phrase level, and the clause level.

The morphemic word consists of a base, combined with (&) or without (shown by parentheses) one or more suffixes, and with a superfix:

$\sqrt{W} = \sqrt[w]{B\&(sf)\&^{\underline{s}}}.$

This constitutes the level of morphology.

The morphemic phrase consists of one or more words combined with a phrase-superfix:

$\sqrt{P} = \sqrt[p]{W_1\&W_2\&\dots W_n,\&^{\underline{ps}}}$

The morphemic clause consists of a morphemic phrase with an intonation pattern:

$\sqrt{Cl} = \sqrt[c]{P\&^{\underline{i}}}.$

Morphemic phrases and clauses are on the level of syntax.

In the analytical procedures of syntax, the syntactic clause, coterminous with the phonemic clause, as stated, and descriptively equivalent to the morphemic clause, is designated by braces and an intonation-pattern symbol: $\{..\}^{\underline{i}}$. When the intonation symbol is removed we are left with a syntactic phrase, equivalent to a morphemic phrase: $\{..\}$. The constituents of such a phrase are called PHRASE FRACTIONS, and are designated by double quotation marks: "..". Phrase-fractions on examination are found to consist of words or portmanteau items. The analysis of clause relations can be made only after the intra-clause analysis is finished; then we can deal with utterances, consisting of one or more clauses:

$$U = Cl_1,\ Cl_2,\ \ldots Cl_n.$$

The utterance written out is in phonemic transcription, which is what we start with originally.

We return now to our illustrative example. In it there are two phonemic clauses, as stated, which we now rewrite as syntactic clauses:

{^{2}lòhŋ+^{3}áylənd^{2}|},

{^{2}iz(+)ə+lôhŋ+^{3}áylənd^{1}#}.

The next step is to remove the intonation patterns, which are, respectively, $\sqrt[i]{}^{2\,3\,2}|$ and $\sqrt[i]{}^{2\,3\,1}\#$. When utterance structures are considered, it will become evident that the sequence of intonation patterns here found, $\sqrt[i]{}^{2\,3\,2}|\&\sqrt[i]{}^{2\,3\,1}\#$, with the first one repeatable up to some small number as yet not determined, is an expansion of the second pattern, which appears alone when the utterance has only one clause. There are other such sequences that can be described and their distribution stated (such as $\sqrt[i]{}^{2\,3}|\&\sqrt[i]{}^{3}||$, found in some questions).

Removing the intonation patterns from the two clauses, we have the syntactic phrases:

{lòhŋ+áylənd}, {iz(+)ə+lôhŋ+áylənd}.

In the first phrase there is one plus-juncture, giving the two phrase-fractions "lohŋ" and "aylənd" and the phrase-superfix √ˋ+ˊ. The two fractions are now identifiable as words of the form ʷ√lóhŋ and ʷ√áylənd; in the presence of the phrase-superfix here found, the first word yields its stress, indicating its structural subordination to the second. The words in question here are identifiable as adjective and noun, respectively, and we have then one of the English adjective-noun constructions. Applying substitution techniques, we find that possible replacements are *Martha's Vineyard* /màhrθəz+vínyərd/, *Madagascar* /mæ̀dəgéhskər/. This adjective-noun construction, then, is syntactically equivalent to some noun-noun constructions, or to a noun (a word, with one base).

In the second phrase above we find a fraction "iz(+)ə", which is identifiable morphemically as composed of ʷ√íz and "ə" (an allolog of ʷ√éy), and the fractions "lohŋ" and "aylənd" with the phrase-superfix √ˆ+ˊ. Once again we have an adjective-noun construction. But on applying substitution techniques, we find that each part takes its own replacements--*short, wide, narrow,* etc., and *peninsula, place, territory,* etc. It becomes clear that the difference between the constructions {lòhŋ+áylənd} and {lôhŋ+áylənd} lies in the superfixes.

In addition to the indicated possible substitutes for {lòhŋ+áylənd}, elements with the superfixes √ˊ+ˆ or √ˊ+ˋ may occur. Examples are in order. In the item *air-raid* we have /éhr+rèyd/. (Since the reference has become rare it may be that many speakers will now say /éhr+rêyd/; it appears to be rather frequently true that items of this kind, with the second part containing one syllable, have √ˊ+ˋ if in very constant use by a speaker, and the rarer ones have √ˊ+ˆ.) Then we add *warden:* /éhr+rèyd+wôhrdən/; here the morpheme appears in the allomorph ᵃ√ˊ+ˋ+ˆ; that is, the dividing point within the morpheme is the /+/ before the /ˆ/. This is borne out on further expansion: *áir+ràid+wàrden+pôst, áir+ràid+wàrden+pòst+stâir+wày* (here *stairway* is itself an item of the type of *air-raid*). At this point expansion of this particular set gives out; further extension requires two phonemic phrases: *áir+ràid+wàrden+pôst|stáir+wày+êntrance.* The application of this to the problem of determining immediate constituents is obvious.

The necessity of working through the several steps in order can be emphasized by consideration of an example having portmanteau items:

I told him I don't know.

said thus /^{2}ày+^{3} tówldɨm^{2}| ^{2}ày+do^{3} nów^{1}#/.

Again removing the intonation patterns $\surd^{232}|^{231}\#$, identical with those of the example above, we have {ày+tówldɨm}, {ày+donów}. The first phrase has the fractions "ay" and "towldɨm". We identify "ay" as $^{w}\surd$áy, the Sg 1 personal pronoun. For the identification of "towldɨm" we use substitution. and by comparison of such fractions as "towldəs", "towldəm", "towldər", etc., we arrive at the conclusion that the apparent word "towldɨm" is composed of $^{w}\surd$tówld followed by an element in normal transition that is a variant of $^{w}\surd$hím; that is, it is an allolog of the Sg3M object pronoun when it comes under the weak stress in a superfix and is in normal transition with what precedes. Our phrase now consists of the words $^{w}\surd$áy, $^{w}\surd$tówld, $^{w}\surd$hím; and the superfix $\surd$ ` + ´˘; this is a common construction of pronoun subject, verb, and pronoun object.

The second phrase, {ày+donów}, has the first fraction "ay" again, once more identified as $^{w}\surd$áy. For the second fraction we find substitutions like {..donwánə}, {..donláykɨt}, and {..dòwn(t)+nów}; also, {..dìdən(t)+nów}, as well as {ày+nów} and {ày+núw}. We identify "now" as $^{w}\surd$nów *know*, a verb. This leads to the identification of "do", as an allolog of "downt", which is itself a portmanteau of $^{w}\surd$dúw and $^{w}\surd$nát. The construction {ày+donów} then consists of the four words $^{w}\surd$áy, $^{w}\surd$dúw, $^{w}\surd$nát, $^{w}\surd$nów, and the phrase superfix $\surd$ ` + ˘ ´; the form of the superfix shows that three of the words are in a portmanteau such that one part of it includes two of them. Only by following each step is it possible to state the constitution of this phrase fully and to describe everything that happens.

4.2. In a phrase like *I don't know* we may have various superfixes: /ày+donów/, /ày+dòwnt+nów/, /ày+dównt+nôw/, /áy+dòwnt+nôw/. The statistically most frequent and most 'neutral' way of saying it is the first; the second is also frequent, especially in 'careful' speech. But the last two are examples of a phenomenon that can be analyzed only as secondary to the first two examples. They exhibit a SHIFT of stress from the 'normal' final position back toward the beginning of the phrase. It may be concluded that there are shift-morphemes, or a shift-morpheme with allomorphs, differing by the position that the primary stress takes in relation to its 'normal' position: $^{a}\sqrt{\ }Sh_{-1}$ ('shift minus one'), $^{a}\sqrt{\ }Sh_{-2}$, etc. In /ày+tówldɨm/ we can get $^{a}\sqrt{\ }Sh_{+1}$, resulting in /ày+tôwld+hím/, since here the 'normal' construction has primary stress on the next-to-the-last element, the pronoun object being under weak stress.

When we compare /àys+kríym/ and /áys+krìym/ for *ice-cream*, we have simply two different dialects. But let us examine such an item as *kitchen-sink:* as a fixture in a kitchen it is called /kìcɨn+síŋk/; if one were taking inventory, one would say /kîcɨn+téybəl/, /kîcɨn+klázɨt/, /kîcɨn+síŋk/; but in contrasting with the laundry sink, one would say /kícɨn+sìŋk/; in the last example we have the shift morpheme again.

Many of the superfixes then, are not limited to one function; √´+^ and √´+` form constructions substitutable for nouns, but are also the result when shift is applied to such a phrase as *Tell John*, giving /tél+jân/, based on a normal /têl+ján/. In constructions involving a verb-adverb phrase, the superfix is basically √`+´; *gèt+úp, sìt+dówn, còme+ín, còme+tó* ('recover consciousness'); this contrasts with √´+` in corresponding noun-like phrases *gét+ùp, sít+dòwn, cóme+òn.*

4.3. In the preceding section reference was made to the morphological classification of various elements. In a language like English it is possible to identify many of tho fraotionc of phrases by their morphology as words of various classes. In doing syntax, then, we identify out the nouns, personal pronouns, adjectives, and verbs, in terms of the criteria established in our morphology. This then enables us to do our substitutions more easily and directly, and to label whole phrases by the resemblance or identity of their functions to those of single words.

We propose the use of terms in *-al* for syntax: NOMINAL, PRONOMINAL, ADJECTIVAL, VERBAL, corresponding to the morphological terms *noun*, *pronoun*, *adjective*, *verb*, and, of course, additional terms as needed--ADVERBIAL, PREPOSITIONAL, etc. The phrase {lòhŋ+áylənd} above is a nominal; the superfix √ + ́ forms, among other things, nominals out of adjectives and nouns, as well as out of nouns and nouns (*ice-cream* /àys+kríym/--for those who say it this way), and other word classes. The contrasting phrase {lǒhŋ+áylənd} is overall nominal in function, also, but is clearly composed of a nominal "aylənd" and an adjectival "lohŋ". If we rank the two constructions, we can call nominals RANK I and adjectivals RANK II. In *a long delayed request* /ə+lòhŋ+dɨlêyd+rɨkwést/, where *request* is the nominal, *long delayed* is adjectival; its constituents are the adjectival *delayed*, and the adverbial, of RANK III, *long*.

In the example *The Pennsylvania Railroad is the main Pennsylvania railroad*, we have: /²ðə+pèn(+)sɨlvèynyə+³réyl+ròwd²|²iz(+)ðə+mêyn+pèn(+)sɨlvêynyə+³réyl+ròwd¹#/. The phrase *The Pennsylvania Railroad* is rank I, a nominal; *the main Pennsylvania railroad* is a complex nominal consisting of two rank II items--*main*, *Pennsylvania*, and the rank I *railroad*. Note also that when an item like *Pennsylvania* is under the tertiary stress of the phrase superfix √ + ́, its two strong stresses become equal. In deliberate or slow speech the complex nominal may be broken up into two or more phonemic phrases, so that the secondary stresses above become primaries:

the+máin|Pènnsylvánia|ráil+rôad.

4.4. The discussion above of ranks of construction also indicates some of the ways in which statements of word order may be made. These must take account of the superfixes and intonation patterns. It will be stated that the sequence verb-adverb, for instance, is verbal with the superfix √ + ́, but nominal with √′+‵; but not all 'adverbs' fit into this pattern, so that the sequence *get there* has √´+ˆ. In a sequence of verb and noun, the usual superfix will be found to be √ˆ+´ : *Ì+sâw+Jóhn;* this superfix also occurs with verb and adverbial: *I lôoked+óut, I lôoked+ínto it, They lêft at níne,* etc. An observation that comes out of this is that the primary stress of a phonemic phrase will come as near the end as possible; here 'as possible' means that some items, such as pronoun objects, certain adverbs, prepositions, and others, do not have primary stress though they are normally the last thing in a phrase, and they get primary stress only with the shift morpheme. The syntactic nature of some items is identifiable by this matter of the order of the stress phonemes: *After an hour she came to.* /...kèym+túw/; *I mean the place we just came to.* /...kéym+tùw/. The first *to* is an adverb, as a part of a verbal; the second we can call a preposition, using as part of the syntactic definition of this class of words the fact that they occur under tertiary stress in constructions of the kind cited. If we now compare *She came too* /...kêym+túw/~/...kéym|túw/, we see how the identification of *too* can also be arrived at--an adverbial following a simple verb.

In order to illustrate how different positions of words in phrases are tied up with the same or different superfixes and how this makes possible syntactic identification, the following examples are presented:

/^{3}nów^1#/
/^{2}ày+^{3}nów^1#/
/^{2}jâ(h)n+^{3}nówz^1#/
/^{2}ày+nôw+^{3}já(h)n^1#/
/^{2}ày+^{3}nów+hìm^1#/ or /^{2}ày+^{3}nówɨm^1#/
/^{2}ày+nôw+^{3}nǽw^1#/
/^{2}šìy+lûks+^{3}sík^1#/
/^{2}šìy + lûks+^{3}sík+næ̂w^1#/. Here /næ̂w/ is a second adverbial and does not have the primary stress, except with shift: /...+sîk+^{3}nǽw^1#/; the regular stress for this construction seems to be /ˆ/, as here.

/²hìyz+gâtə+lôw+slə̀ŋ+³káhr¹#/

/ ²hìyz+gâtə+lòw+slə̂ŋ+³káhr¹#/ This example and the preceeding are probably in free alternation.

/²hìyz+gâtə+lòw+slə̀ŋ+³káhr¹#/

/²hìz+³káhr²| ²wəz+lòw+³slə́ŋ¹#/

/²ðə+³búk²| ²iz+wèl+³rítɨn¹#/

/ ²ðə+³búk²| ²iz+rîtɨn+³wél¹#/ In these last two examples the first has a unitary adjectival construction, /wèl+rítɨn/, the second has verb followed by adverb.

In summary, the points illustrated are: position of primary stress at the end of a phonemic phrase in most constructions; the superfix as a former of unitary constructions of one kind or another; stress distributions on sequences of adverbials and adjectivals; syntactic function indicated by order of stresses as well as order of words; intonation normally tied up with stress so that /³/ occurs coincidentally with /ʹ/.

It can be seen that with the procedures suggested here, such questions as 'Is *back* an adjective or a noun in *back door*?' 'Is *home* an adverb in *I'm going home*?', and so on, become essentially meaningless, and really pertinent questions about the constructions can be asked and answered.

We have not considered questions relating to the order of words within phrases, the agreements between clauses or parts of clauses, and many other items treated in the traditional syntax. On the whole, such matters have been dealt with, at least for the literary language, at length and rather well in many studies. The chief objection that might be made would be to point out that metalinguistic or even philosophical considerations have not always been excluded.

The contribution of the phonological analysis of stress, juncture, and intonation patterns, of the morphological analysis of superfixes, and of the identification of allologs to syntactic analysis is not that this eliminates or replaces part-of-speech syntax, the recognition of immediate constituents, and the discussions of the kind just mentioned, but that it makes these techniques into solidly established objective procedures, removing once and for all the necessity of defending one's subjective judgments as to what goes with what.

4.5. An aspect of English syntax that is involved in such a phrase as {ày+donów} is the matter of VERBAL PHRASES. These are important enough methodologically to warrant examination here.

In what follows, the ordinary orthographic forms will be used, and attention will be called to the actual phonemic forms only occasionally. But in these verb phrases it is precisely the superfixes that make units of them and give them their functional identity in larger constructions.

The inflectional forms of a normal English verb (cf. 3.5) are the common form, the Sg3 non-past, the past, the past participle, and the present participle. These may be symbolized as follows: V, VZ^3, VD^1, VD^2, Viŋ. Syntactically, V and VZ^3 are in complementary distribution in the 'simple present' construction--*I, you, we go* as against *he, she it goes*; we shall accordingly symbolize this as $V(Z^3)$. The constructions of $V(Z^3)$ contrast in similar (though not identical) frames with those of VD^1. The labels 'simple present' and 'simple past' respectively, are neither better nor worse than any others in common use for these forms. However, to avoid certain connotations of the term *present*, we shall call them NON-PAST and PAST respectively. These two forms will be called the TENSES. There are only two tenses, then, in English, and all verbs --the defective ones as well as the normal ones--have the two forms. All other finite verb constructions are phrases, involving an AUXILIARY verb and one of the forms V, VD^2, Viŋ.

Constructions with Viŋ are formed with the $V(Z^3)$ and VD^1 forms of *be: is going, were going*. The somewhat parallel forms with *keep--keeps going, kept going*--do not, in standard speech, ever occur with less than tertiary stress on *keep, kept*, and are therefore not to be included here, since the controlling criterion is the presence of a weak-stressed allolog of the auxiliary except when shift is involved. The construction with *be* may be labelled the DURATIVE ASPECT, having the two tenses, non-past and past. The construction with *keep*, and the parallel one with *start*, and such others as may exist, can be called aspect-like, and given special labels, if one wishes. The caution is given here that the labels suggested are of minimal importance in the exposition.

Next we have constructions of *have*, *had* with VD²: *has gone*, *had gone*. These may be called the non-past and past PERFECT. With some verbs constructions with *be* and VD² appear in similar frames: *I'm done, they're gone.* These may be called the RESULTATIVE. Perfect and resultative will be called PHASES.

The perfect and the durative may combine--*I've been going.*

Then we have constructions with *shall*, *will*, *may*, *can*, *dare*, *need*, and V: *we shall go*, *we will go*, *I might go*, *he can go*. The first four show non-past and past; *dare* and *need* appear only in a very limited number of uses (negative and interrogative chiefly--see below). In addition to these we find *do (does)*, *did* with V. In all of these, the superfix structure is extremely important: *I'll go* ⫽àhl+gów⫽, *I can do it* /ày(+)kɨn+dúwɨt/, *they do know* /ðèy+dúw+nôw/, etc. These constructions will be called the MODES: the *shall-should* mode, the *will-would* mode (this could be labelled FUTURE--the allolog /‿(ə)l/ belongs here), the *can-could* mode, the *may-might* mode, the *do-did* mode. The last has been called 'emphatic', but it is the superfix that makes it emphatic, not the auxiliary: *they do know* and *they will know* /ðèy+wíl+nôw/ are equally emphatic: and in the negative there is nothing emphatic except in the superfix: /ðèy+dòwn(t)+nów/--/ðèy+dównt+nôw/. The word *must* enters into similar constructions, but since it has no inflection, it should not be labelled a verb; it can be called an uninflected verbal, and its constructions can be identified as mode-like. In considering how to classify *better* in *I better go*, we take into account the free alternation with *I'd better go*, and such responses as *You better had*, and conclude that there is involved in the first example a zero allolog of *had*, and that *better* is not a verbal.

The modes combine with both phases and aspects in the sequences (M = modal auxiliary) M *be* Viŋ, M *have* VD^2, M *have been* Viŋ.

Similar to the modes are constructions with *be*, *have* (and the uninflected verbal *ought*) combined with V preceded by *to*: *am to go*, *have to go*, *ought to go*. Here *to* is almost always under /˘/ in a superfix; with *have* the allologic forms are /hǽftə/, /hǽstə/, /hǽdə/, with basic superfix √´˘. Then there is *want to*, usually /wán(t)ə/; and the durative mode of *go*, with *to* and V: *I'm going to go* /àym+gònə+gów/ (also /gə́nə/, /góyntə/, /gówɨn+tə/, and other allologic forms). In these constructions all or most of the possible phrasal expansions of *want* and *go* may be found; this is also true for *have*. Constructions with *let* and *make*, without *to*, but with the goal inserted between auxiliary and verb, are also similar to the modes: *let him go*, *make him do it*.

Next we have constructions with *be* and VD^2: *it was done*. This is called the PASSIVE VOICE.

It can be combined with most of the constructions previously listed. *Get* enters into voice-like constructions, but does not ever have weak stress.

Finally may be noted constructions in which the subject of the auxiliary follows it (INTERROGATIVE), and those in which some allolog of *not* follows the auxiliary (NEGATIVE). These are the STATUSES. The simple forms $V(Z^3)$ and VD^1 do not occur in these statuses in modern English, their place in frames being taken by the *do*-mode.

A summary of the verbal phrases discussed, for the verb *see*, follows in *Sg3M:*

	Non-past tense:	*Past tense:*
simple:	*he sees*	*he saw*
durative aspect:	*he is seeing*	*he was seeing*
perfect phase:	*he has seen*	*he had seen*
perfect durative:	*he has been seeing*	*he had been seeing*
shall mode:	*he shall see*	*he should see*
will-mode:	*he will see*	*he would see*
may-mode	*he may see*	*he might see*
can-mode	*he can see*	*he could see*
do-mode	*he does see*	*he did see*
will-mode durative:	*he will be seeing*	*he would be seeing*
will-mode perfect:	*he will have seen*	*he would have seen*
have to:	*he has to see*	*he had to see*
going to:	*he's going to see*	*he was going to see*
passive voice:	*he is seen*	*he was seen*
interrogative status:	*does he see*	*did he see*
negative status:	*he doesn't see*	*he didn't see*

PART III: METALINGUISTICS

5.1. The statement has been made many times that the rigid techniques followed for the analysis of linguistic systems should not be extended to include considerations of the meaning of the elements classified. Considerations of this nature have generally been relegated to the sociologist, the ethnologist, or the philologist. At the same time, however, linguists have based various elementary definitions on meaning, and have usually used meaning to a greater or less extent in all linguistic procedures. Thus, the morpheme has been defined hitherto in terms of meaning, and all the work done to date in syntax could be termed 'meaning syntax'. The procedure followed in this *Outline* has endeavored to use the meaning of recurring partials only as a short cut to the establishing of contrasting structural features, as pointed out in 4, and to go forward on the assumption that microlinguistic analysis can and must deal with statements about the distributions of the elements rigidly observed on ascending levels of complexity of organization.

The realization of the extreme importance of levels in the observation and classification of events in the whole field of human behavior has been and will doubtless continue to be one of the most important criteria for scientific work in the social sciences. By the same token, failure to separate and classify data properly in this regard has been one of the main weaknesses of much of what has been done not only in linguistics but in all the social sciences to date. It is probably true that in linguistics, because of the extremely formal and handleable nature of the data, the greatest progress in organization on the proper levels has been made.

As mentioned in 0.2, after a complete microlinguistic analysis has been made, further considerations can occupy the attention of the investigator, in the area termed metalinguistics. This can be said to include the overall relation of the linguistic system to the other systems of the cultural totality. This area, with prelinguistics and microlinguistics, completes the whole field, referred to as MACROLINGUISTICS.

Metalinguistics includes the various matters often referred to as 'ethnolinguistics' (cf. D. L. Olmsted, Ethnolinguistics so far, *SIL:OP2*[1950]), but is far more inclusive. Not only does it deal with WHAT people talk about and WHY, but also considers HOW they use the linguistic system, and how they react to its use. This leads further to the consideration of how the linguistic system affects the behavior, both conscious and unconscious, and the world-view of the speaker, and governs or influences the interactions between individuals and between groups. Linguistic behavior is, by definition, part of the overt culture, but the study of it as metalinguistics shows it to be not only a guide to the covert culture but, in large part, the structural framework itself of the covert culture or sentiment-structure.

Metalinguistics may be considered in terms of subdivisions paralleling those of microlinguistics--METALINGUISTIC PHONOLOGY and METALINGUISTIC MORPHEMICS--as well as in overall terms. The overall approach was first outlined by B. L. Whorf (cf. *Four articles on metalinguistics*, Washington, D.C., Foreign Service Institute, Department of State, 1950--a reprint of: Science and linguistics, *Technology Review* 42,6 [1940]; Linguistics as an exact science, *ibid.* 43,2 [1940]; Languages and logic, *ibid.* 43,6 [1941]; The relation of habitual thought and behavior to language, *Language, culture, and personality* [Sapir memorial volume, Menasha, Wisconsin, 1941]; see also Whorf's An American Indian model of the universe, *IJAL* 16.67-72 [1950]).

5.2. Metalinguistic phonology treats of the variations in use of allophones and phonemes and the reaction of different individuals or groups to such varying usages.

There are current in popular literature allusions to 'Brooklynese' or 'honey-chile' accents, to Scotch 'burrs', to Midwestern 'harshness' or 'slurring'. The difference between these designations and the linguist's identification of local dialects lies in the differing levels at which the material is considered. The linguist, as micro-linguist, goes into a community 'cold'; he knows nothing about the culture, nor does he care; he starts by selecting an informant, most often on the basis of finding someone--anyone--who has the time to work with him, and analyzes that informant's speech. When the linguist has made his microlinguistic statements, for one or many informants, then he can, if he wishes, begin operating on the metalinguistic level. He can take the reactions of various speakers to each other's speech, and attempt to tie up these reactions with sociological facts of one kind or another. The remark that someone speaks 'well' or 'crudely' or 'with a Brooklyn accent' is a datum: the metalinguist can turn it into a conclusion by clearly identifying out the microlinguistic characteristics of the speech, and then correlating them with the speaker's social class, his status in the community, the reactions of others to him, and so on. If one speaker says /hǽnd/ for *hand*, and another says /héhnd/, there is first a microlinguistic identification to be made of the local dialects involved. But then it may be that in the particular area being studied /hǽnd/ is found in a part of town that is economically more favored than the locality where /héhnd/ predominates; the description of the situation is metalinguistics, on a microlinguistic basis. But suppose, as is actually the case in some areas, that *hand* is phonemically always /héhnd/; however, some speakers have, for /eh/, the phonetic events summarized as [ɛ˅ə̣], while others have [ɛ̣˅ˑə̂]; the characterization of the latter set of allophones as 'inelegant' can only be made on the basis of the correlation of the microlinguistic facts with other cultural systems, that is, it can only be done as metalinguistics.

Further elaboration of the kinds of material treatable under metalinguistic phonology, with tentative analyses of preliminary observations of reactions to regional and class differences, must be left to separate articles.

5.3. Metalinguistic morphemics treats of the variations in use of allomorphs and morphemes and the reaction of different individuals or groups to such varying usages. This statement is meant to include the use of ALL the allomorphs and morphemes and the reaction to them; that is, metalinguistic morphemics deals with all the meanings of linguistic forms as ordinarily understood, as well as the 'meanings' that identify 'standard' and 'substandard' forms and the like.

Consider the utterances *He was awe-struck* and *He was grief-stricken*. The analysis of the forms *struck* and *stricken* must, of course, start with the microlinguistic morphology. The interesting and striking fact then emerges, that on the MICROLINGUISTIC MORPHOLOGICAL LEVEL both *struck* and *stricken* are base $\sqrt{}$strayk- combined with suffix $\sqrt{}$-D^2 (cf. 3.5); in the first case $\sqrt{}$-D^2 has the allomorph $\sqrt[a]{}$(ay>ə) -∅, in the second it has $\sqrt[a]{}$(ay>i) -ɨn. When levels are not separated, all kinds of difficulties arise from an example like this, and questions are asked as to how many morphemes --base or suffix--there are. However, when it is realized that in the microlinguistic testing frame *struck* and *stricken* are equivalents, then it is seen that the analysis of the meaning-difference between them is chiefly metalinguistic. We say chiefly because on the microlinguistic level statements of morpheme-distribution can be made (*struck* with *awe*, *stricken* with *grief*, and so on).

The gradations and varieties of reaction in this field can be indicated by mention of a few other past participle forms. The use of *dived* and *dove* is much less reacted to than that of *struck* and *stricken*; *dived* and *dove* are freely substitutable for each other; the slight connotation of greater literary elegance in *dived* is the only metalinguistic datum here. In the case of *drunk* as a past participle another metalinguistic element enters, that of tabu; *I have drunk it* is standard, but many educated speakers will recast their sentences, and say, possibly, *I've had it to drink*, or (facetiously or with conscious elegance), *I've imbibed it*; the insecure and less educated speaker will say *I have drank it*, and worry about or stumble over the form. As a final instance, *I have knowed* can be called substandard or 'incorrect'.

The instances just cited are examples of the use of different PARALOGS, a paralog being one of the forms constituting an inflectional paradigm. Other instances of the use of different paralogs are the colloquial *It's me* as against the literary *It is I*, and the hyperurbanism *Between you and I* for the standard *Between you and me.* On the other hand the use of *them* for *those* is an instance of different morpheme distribution and the metalinguistic reaction to it.

The difference between *I feel bad* and *I feel badly* is microlinguistically simply a difference between two constructions. Preliminary observations made by us lead to the tentative metalinguistic conclusion that in some regions the one or the other of these forms is reacted to as non-standard, or possibly simply as a regional difference.

As we have shown in our microlinguistic analyses, the stress phonemes, juncture phonemes, and pitch phonemes are used in English as parts of superfixes and intonation patterns, these being morphemes. On the microlinguistic level, it was preeminently clear that the analysis of these entities as morphemes was in no way dependent on their meaning. As far as we can now see, superfixes have no meanings except such microlinguistic ones as 'word with three vocalic nuclei', 'phrase of two words', including the syntactic meanings 'nominal unit construction', 'verb-object construction', and the like. Intonation patterns, however, do have meanings, and, when they have been described microlinguistically, it is possible to begin to examine these meanings. Compare *What are we having for dinner, Mother?* with *What are we having for dinner--steak?* The pattern $\sqrt{}^{2}\|$ on *Mother* might be called one of the forms of the 'vocative', while $\sqrt{}^{3}\|$ on *steak* is part of the intonation of questions of certain kinds. The interchange of these two patterns gives ludicrous results because of the incongruousness with possible cultural situations, pointing up clearly that the meaning analysis is not on the level of microlinguistic morphemics.

The reactions to the differences between ^{2}*Hôw dŏ thèy* ^{3}*stúdy*^{1}# and ^{3}*Hôw* ^{2}*dŏ thěy stúdy*$\|$, or between ^{3}*Jóhnny*^{2}#

and ^{3}*Jóhnny* ^{2}||, or ^{2}*Jóhn* ^{3}*ny#* and ^{2}*Jóhn* ^{3}*ny* || (and there is also ^{3}*Jóhnny* ^{1}*#*), are examinable under another part of metalinguistic morphemics, that concerned with regional, class, status, and similar differences.

5.4. At the end of our treatment of microlinguistic phonology (1.8), some remarks were made about certain kinds of phenomena that were to be considered as metalinguistics, under the heading of style.

Without attempting to define style rigidly, we may at this point mention all the kinds of phenomena we would include under it. First, then, there are the phenomena mentioned in 1.8 --increased loudness, extra high or extra low pitch, accompanied often by drawling or stretching out of the whole of an utterance. These, along with all matters of tempo and tone of voice, can be called by a technical term--DISTORTION.

Any analysis of the conditions under which distortion takes place is metalinguistic. In the statements about it, there will have to be pointed out the possibilities available, and the choice made. Distortion is then a result of stylistic SELECTION. From this it is fairly clear that all the other matters of style which will be mentioned are also results of selection. Included are: so-called free variation (such as the selection of released allophones of final stops); the variation in the use of phonemes in particular items (/gríysiy/ and /gríyziy/ from the same speaker); the use of *dived* vs. *dove*; the selection of constructions--simple vs. complex; the choice of vocabulary items (*evil* instead of *bad*).

It is our belief that the phenomena alluded to are not only worthy of study but can actually be studied and analyzed by developing appropriate metalinguistic techniques. We do not believe, however, that anything but the most tentative stylistic analyses can be made as yet. And we emphasize that even the first tentative attempts can only be made in terms of a rigid separation of levels and an understanding that the microlinguistic analysis must precede and be as full as possible.

5.5. It is clear from the brief statement about style hat we become concerned, in dealing with it, with the verall problem of the relation of the linguistic system o the rest of the culture.

The analysis of this problem must rest upon foundaions that do not yet exist: not only must the whole marolinguistic analysis be available, at least in outline, ut there must be at hand analyses of all the significant tructures in the culture of the speakers of the language. nglish being a language spoken by a very great number of eople, of many diverse subcultures (or even actually culures as such), and culturological science having as yet ealt very little with such complex societal structures, t is obvious that the problem can only be posed and some uggestions made as to possible fields of investigation ithin it.

The unstated assumptions of a societal structure, and ts overall value systems, can be assumed to reflect and e reflected in the language, and Sapir and Whorf have ade a number of valuable suggestions in this connection. f course, it would be much too facile a conclusion that a ertain kind of linguistic system 'makes' a society go in or science, or for belief in certain myths, or for one nalysis of physical phenomena as against another. We erely suggest that certain linguistic structures and cerain other cultural structures may reinforce and strengthn each other in ways worthy of investigation. Here again he matter of levels must be emphasized: we had better be retty sure of our ground in microlinguistic analysis and he parts of metalinguistics alluded to already, as well s in the ethnological material under consideration, beore trying to do this kind of work.

In our culture dichotomizing is very common. It ight be worth investigating how this is related to the inguistic pairing of such words as *good* and *bad*, *right* nd *wrong*, *clean* and *dirty*, etc.. For most effects we seek auses, often in terms of the fallacy of *post hoc, ergo ropter hoc*; is this reinforced by or does it reinforce the linguistic prevalence of the actor-action-goal con structions? These questions are very broad, indeed. Bu there are much more limited ones that can be examined. Ho is the world view as to colors of a man who knows onl *green* and *blue* different from that of his wife who ca tell *chartreuse* from *aquamarine* as well, and what effec does this difference, if any, have on what they write o how they behave? The behavior of persons who know al about their *fifth cousins twice removed* is certainly dif ferent in respect to relatives from that of those wh don't even know what a *second cousin* is. Is this in an way tied up with the linguistic facts--or is there any re lation between the two factors? Does the fact that w say *cup of coffee* as /kə̀pə+kóhfiy/ and *student of Englis* as /stùwdəntəv+íngliš/, influence the educator who object to or favors, as the case may be, 'pouring knowledge' int his charges?

Many more such suggestions could be made. We hope t expand on them in a more appropriate place.

APPENDICES

6.1. There is presented here an alphabetical list of echnical terms that are defined or described in the pre-eeding text. However, phonetic and phonemic terms that re in current use and that are developed at length in the iscussion are not included, nor are terms that constitute, y themselves, section headings in the table of contents--nless the term itself is introduced earlier than the sec-ion heading. Reference numbers are to sections.

6.2. The following list of symbols and formulas i[s] complete, except that combinations of more than one symbo[l] are exemplified but are not listed in full. The first ap-pearance of each symbol or group of symbols is indicate[d] by the section number in parentheses.

Phonetic symbols are inclosed in brackets, [ ], i[n] the text. They are:

Vowels and vowel modifiers: i I e E æ ɨ ɨ ə ɜ a u̇ U̇ Ï Ë . ɑ u U o Ω ɔ ω ɒ ˆ ˇ < > ‚ ˆ : ˙ ˚ ˘ ⊓ ⊔ ˆ ɚ w (1).

Consonants and consonant modifiers: p t k b d g f θ s š ð z ž m n ŋ l ʻ ¬ · ˘ ƙ ś ṣ š č ǰ ə x y P T K ŧ ʔ t r¹ ŋ̆g ɹ + ˆ (1). ɖ ɠ ɣ (etc.) i i u (etc.) l (1.4).

Phonemic symbols are inclosed in slant-lines,/ /, i[n] the text. They are:

Vowels: i e æ ɨ ə a u o ɔ (1.31).

Cover symbols: V F B C (1.32).

Semivowels: y w h (1.32).

Consonants: p t k b d g c j f θ s š v ð z ž m n ŋ l r (1.5).

Stress symbols: [ˈ ˘ ˘ ˘], /ˊ ˘ ˋ ˆ/ (1.61). [ˆ] (1.62).

Juncture symbols: ˬ /+/ (1.62). /| || #/ (1.72).

Pitch symbols: [↓ $\overset{1}{\circ}$ $\overset{1}{\wedge}$ $\overset{1}{\perp}$ $\overset{2}{\vee}$] etc., [¨ + ¯], /^{1} ^{2} ^{3} ^{4}/ (1.71).

Examples (a)-(e), (aa)-(ee), (f)-(q) in phonemic transcription (1.8).

Morphemic symbols: $\surd$ - (2.11). & → $\overset{w}{\surd}$ $\overset{ps}{\surd}$ $\overset{p}{\surd}$ (2.12). ← (2.13). $\overset{a}{\surd}$~ (3). -Z^1 -s_2 -ɨz_2 -z_2 -Ø ($\tilde{V}$)-Ø ^{L} (is>iyz) (əs>ay) (ə>iy) -Z^2 (3.2). Pronoun morphemes: (3.3). -ər -ɨst (3.4). -Z^3 -z_2 -Ø -D^1 -t -d -t_2 -t_3 -d_2 -D^2 -(ə)n -iŋ (3.5). Forms of *be:* (3.5). ´ ´˘^{2} ´˘˘^{3} (3.6).

Syntactic symbols: $\{..\}^{\underline{i}}$ $\{..\}$ $\overset{i}{\surd}$ (4.1). $\overset{a}{\surd}Sh_{-1}$ $\overset{a}{\surd}Sh_{-2}$ $\overset{a}{\surd}Sh_{+1}$ (4.2). V VZ^3 VD^1 VD^2 Viŋ M (4.5).

Formulas (4.1): /W/ = /Ph_{seg}, Ph_{str}/. /P/ = /Ph_{seg}, Ph_{str}, +/. /Cl/ = /P, Ph_{pi}, Ph_{tj}/. $\surd W$ = $\overset{w}{\surd}$B&(sf)&$^{\underline{s}}$. $\surd P$ = $\overset{p}{\surd}W_1$&W_2&...W_n, &$^{\underline{ps}}$. $\surd Cl$ = $\overset{c}{\surd}$P&$^{\underline{i}}$. U = Cl_1, Cl_2, ...Cl_n.